Love
LEAPS FORWARD

(UNTIL DO WE PART)

TIME TILTS BACKWARD

Love
LEAPS
FORWARD
(UNTIL DO WE PART)
TIME TILTS BACKWARD

RETHA EVANS EZELL, J. CALVIN EZELL

Contents

Special Tribute..1
Endorsement (Reviews)..2
His Foreword 9
My Foreword 11
Dedication 14
Introduction..17

SECTION ONE: TIME TILTS BACKWARD......................21
My Town..23
A Backward Glance 25
My Aunt And Uncle's Place..30
My Aunt And Uncle's Place (Original Poem) 33
Oh My: Where To Now?..35
Life Without Father 40
My Father And I (Original Poem) 46
There's No Place Like Home..48
My Mother Wasn't (Original Poem) 52

SECTION TWO: TIME TO MAKE FRIENDS......................53
Peanuts (Trisha)! Popcorn (Emma) And Cracker
Jacks! (Rete) 55
The Letter 61
Love Is In The Air 64
Gone Too Soon 67
My Friend And I (Original Poem) 71
Life Is Challenging: The World Is Changing 73
Grandmothers (Original Poem) 83

SECTION THREE: LOVE LEAPS FORWARD 85
Welcome To Adulthood..88
One Nation Under God (Original Poem)..................................93
Off To The City 94

Time To Move Forward..98
I Believe In Miracles!..102
Building Our Nest...106
For Better Or For Worse...109
In Sickness And In Health...116
Faith In A Fig?...118
Lord, You Send Me A Jew 121
The Examination 125
Gifted Hands 129
Do It Again, Lord...133
Near Death Experience? 138
Who Can Help Me? 143

SECTION FOUR: THE SPIRITUAL JOURNEY..................................149
The Calling...151
The Ordination..156
The Assignments...160
First Sunday Morning 166
A Very Blessed Day 168
My Other Assignment...170

SECTION FIVE: HERE WE STAND 175
Here We Stand And He Still Gives Me Butterflies...........................177
Behold New Things Shall Come (Original Poem) 182

Epilogue..184
Appendix..190
Did You Know?...192
Marriage (Q.U.I.C.K.) 194
Acknowledgments 199
Special Acknowledgment..201

Love Leaps Forward

(Until Death Do We Part)

Time Tilts Backward

For you are my hope O Lord God;

You are my trust from my youth.

By You I have been upheld from birth;

You are He who took me out of my mother's womb.

My praise shall be continually of you.

Psalm 71:5 - 6

Time Tilts Backward

To everything there is a season,

A time for every purpose under heaven:

A time to be born

And a time to die…

Ecclesiastes 3:1-2

SPECIAL TRIBUTE

In Loving memory
of my husband
James Calvin Ezell
You left this world but not my heart

Now she who is really a widow, and left alone, trusts in God and continues in supplications and prayers night and day. *I Timothy 5:5*

To My God,

My Creator, Maker, whom I love faithfully with all my heart, with all my soul, and with all my mind. *Matthew 22:37*

And

His Son, and the word of God that is embedded in my heart, through the Holy Spirit, which has brought me to this place in my life to joyfully accept the endearing end of my *marriage covenant* with my earthly husband. God has "*now*" called me out of my widowhood, and has laid my stones with colorful gems, and my foundation with sapphires, and made my pinnacles of rubies, and my gates of crystals and all my walls of precious stones, and all my children are taught of the Lord. Great shall be the peace of my children. In righteousness, I shall be established, for you God have restored unto me promises and blessings (as You did Israel.) *Isaiah 54:11-1*

"Unto You, I *now* pledge Thee my troth." *Isaiah 54:5*

Endorsement (Reviews)

First Edition:

"This powerful story, infused with original poetry that punctuates key themes, is a breath of fresh air! The vivid details underscore the author's love for each other and the Lord. Each chapter compels you to ponder your own relationship and propels you to take a walk down the memory lanes of love and life. Truly love does "*leap forward*"."

—Andrew & Danese Turner, childhood sweethearts and married for 20 years; Danese is the author and producer of numerous stage plays, including *Blood Relatives* and *Big and Bud*

"Retha is able to capture the readers through the stories of her life and the lives of those she loves. Her journey is a true testament of the goodness and mercies of God."

—Stormy Denison, author of *Single and Depressed: Yeah Right!* and *Pushed by the Winds*

"I just re-read the first edition of "Love Leaps Forward, Time Tilts Backward" and I am now waiting for the revised copy to be published. I had many take- aways from the first book:

Real love and true love will last forever

No problem is too great or too small for the one true and living God

God's will shall be done in sickness, sorrow, sin, and pain and the enemy can't prevent them."

—Pastor Lizzie Germany
Devoted Member- Walking in Grace Fellowship,
Macon, GA (Pastor Robert Zeigler Jr.)

"For a few months leading up to when I re-read *Love Leaps Forward: Time Tilts Backward*, I'd thought about the book a couple of times and felt a need to pick it back up again. I didn't realize it then, but now I know the urge I felt was a prompt from God. Re-reading this collection of stories and life experiences exemplified divine timing in many ways. Every now and then I need a fresh perspective of how sovereign God is, how much and how deeply He loves us, and how precious life is...this was one of those moments when I encountered all of this and more. His sovereignty, providence, and faithfulness are overarching themes of this book and the unified life of this couple. You'll see this as you explore the book's pages. It's more than a re-telling of circumstances; it's a collection of reflections that have taken me on a journey filled with swift transitions and that caused me to wonder what would happen next. Even in the midst of recalling different life events, the author has a positive outlook and focuses on what she can be grateful for while being honest about feelings of sadness and surprise. She looks at life from a place of abundance, not deficit, and I love how she weaves in nuggets of wisdom while doing so. Not only is food for thought sprinkled throughout the book, but so are glimpses of how our society used to be in the past. What's amazing is that the book is still, and maybe even more so, relatable even after it was first published 10 years ago.

Change is constant, but so is God. This book contains so many glimpses of how God orchestrated two lives to live as one for His glory and how there is no such thing as coincidence. As an eye witness to their devotion to the Lord and each other my whole life, reading the book strengthened my faith and increased my desire to follow in the Ezells' footsteps of having a life defined by prayer and obedience. The wonderful thing about the author is that she shows how The Author operates outside of time and has love that endures forever, which means that He can make His plan and purpose for anyone's life come to pass. So, be encouraged, and if you feel the Lord tugging on your heart to read this book or do anything related to its contents, I'll share what the author tells me all the time, *hop to it*! Let God renew your mind and transform you and your legacy, just as he did for Mr. and Mrs. Ezell."

—Goddaughter, Nekeisha Lynne Randall
Devoted Member- Cornerstone Church,
Athens, GA (Pastor Scott Sheppard)
UGA Athens, Doctoral Student

First Draft:

This little "composition book" was lost before the first
edition was finished. It dropped off my husband's bookshelf
a month ago and was probably providentially hidden in
reserve just for this revised edition. I laughed because I always
was his "Spill-Chick", and he was my "Math Champ!".
Somehow, we always seemed to complement each other.
<u>PRICELESS!</u>

Forward (Foreword) ☺

It's amazing how God put People together. I did'nt know her but she knew me. She said she knew I was the one she was going to marry when I spoke on an assembly program in Elementary school., this was in the 4th grade. I did'nt know her or even remember meeting her and then it happen almost a year after she said(he's the one.)

She was walking through a pathway that the kids used for a short cut from one street to the next. She was wearing a blouse with little flowers red shorts and sandles, she and her younger sister was dressed a like. My wife and I sister was coming to visit her friend who was my puppy love girl friend.

After while we became friends, friendship turn in to love, love into Marrage that been over 41 years ago.

In any relationship there going to be some Ups and downs some Trials and Tribulations. Our Marrietal Vows have been tried. Our Ministry, our income, Our health but through grace and Mercy. When we did'nt know God he was watching over us That a why we are still standing today. Love for one another but most of all for God (over)

God is to wise to make a mistake
Scripture (if God is for you who can
be against you)
God not only ordain marrage, he
Also Ordains relationships
I Thank you Lord for leading
her in the path to meet me but
Most of All leading her in the
path of rightousness for your
name sake

Love you Retha E 16

HIS FOREWORD

(2013)

It is amazing how God knows how to put people together when they have been called according to His purpose. When I met "Rete" (Retha), I didn't know her but she knew me. She said she knew I was the one she was going to marry when we were just in the fourth grade. I caught her eye at our elementary school assembly program when I was reciting: "Give Me Liberty or Give Me Death", a poem by Patrick Henry.

"Rete", as I affectionately call her, lived on the same side of town that I lived. She lived on the street in front of mine and I lived on what was known as "back" street. I met her one day as she and her sister were walking through a path that connected our two streets together. Rete was coming to visit her friend, Margie, who just happened to be my "puppy love" girlfriend.

In time, Rete and I lost contact for a few years. Then, my "puppy love" girlfriend moved right across from her. Rete and I began seeing each other regularly whenever she came over to visit her friend. Everything changed when we began seeing each other on a regular basis. Our friendship turned into courtship and finally, our courtship turned into marriage. Once our paths crossed, we found ourselves walking hand in hand even to this day. In the year 2013, we celebrated our forty-second wedding anniversary. In any relationship there are going to be ups and downs.

We had our share of trials and tribulations. Together, we have experienced it all: family, finances, children, hurts, disappointments, ill health, and even a very special and unique ministry that we share together.

But God was always watching over us. His grace and His mercy kept us. This is the reason we are standing together today with everlasting love in our hearts for one another, but most of all, for God.

God is omniscient. He knows all things. He knows our beginning and our end. There is a familiar song and a fitting scripture that sums up our relationship to God and each other. The song asks the question: "If it had not been for the Lord on our side where would we be?" The scripture found in Romans 8 asks the question: "Who shall separate us from the love of Christ? (Or even from each other). Shall tribulation, or distress, or persecution, or famine, or nakedness, or peril or sword?" We say nay, none of these things.

Rete, I thank God that we were more than conquerors through Him who loved us. Rete, I thank God for leading you down the path to meet me but most of all I thank Him for leading us down the path of righteousness for His namesake. *"I am blessed in knowing that our love will never end, but it will one day transcend when we both meet our Lord face to face."*

Love,
Calvin

MY FOREWORD

(2023)

This "revised edition" of Love Leaps Forward, Time Tilts Backward", *(Until Death Do We Part)* is dedicated in loving memory of my husband, (James Calvin Ezell), who not only shared in writing the chapters in our first edition, but lovingly supported me in the revised edition, which covers the final seasons of our lives together, as husband and wife. After fifty-two (52) years of marriage, the leaves continued to turn and the seasons were forever changing. And in spite of all of our ups and downs, we managed to enjoy a happy and fulfilling life through our faith in the living God, and our daily communion with Holy Spirit.

We continued to face each day in love, joy and hope, peacefully waiting in heavenly anticipation, for that day when the chapters of this book of our life together would be closed. Though we both knew it was inevitable, I must admit, it happened a lot sooner than I expected. But I know it was according to God's will and plan for our lives. I truly believe on Thursday, September 14, 2023, when my husband restfully closed his eyes in peace, we had fulfilled God's plan for His Creation (***Genesis 1:27-28)*** through our lives, as husband and wife according to His covenant of marriage, *"Until death do, we part."*

I count it a blessing, that my husband and I were able to take our last "leap of faith and love" as we journeyed together, in revising our book. As I sat typing, I showed him the first edition, he held it in his hand, and smiled. I am sure, even in his illness, he understood. Being in the same room with me, he listened to and heard most of my conversations with the publishing consultants. He heard the names of Trisha and Jess many times, he was aware of the cost, and even knew the name, "Reader's Magnet", which by the way is an amazing publishing company!

Throughout my husband's illness, by the grace of God, he was by my side, inspiring and encouraging me, as I toiled over finishing the last revisions of our book. From beginning to end, he has always been an integral part of this journey. During his illness, he graciously provided me space. Even in his last hour, through his endearing love, long suffering, perseverance and humble spirit, and through his faith and life testimonies, *I Peter 5:6-11* I was able to make all the necessary revisions needed to make "our story" complete.

Throughout this journey, he lovingly supported me from his bedside, or sometimes, as he sat at the computer in a chair, beside me. One night, he even picked up the pages and began to read them. Early mornings, as I typed, he would pass by and gently pat me on my shoulder, and give me a few words of love and a "vote of confidence", gently speaking, "You'll make it!"

On September 7th, just a week before he passed, as I knelt praying, he sat up in his bed. I felt his arms around me and he began to pray a very long and powerful prayer filled with love and thanksgiving. He was thanking God for His goodness, and me for all I had done for him, especially, during his illness. His last words were whispered very softly, pausing after every word, "Listen", *You... have... done... a... great... job...!* You... will... be... fine...!

Immediately, he laid down, closed his eyes and slept peacefully. The next few days, the family gathered around his bed and watched in "glorified hope", as he very quietly eased into his eternal rest. Unequivocally, he had lived out his favorite quote *"It is well with my soul!"*

I had just finished my last chapter of the revision of our book, as he closed out the last chapter of his life.

Over the years, I am convinced more than ever that love does leap forward and time does seem to tilt backward, on occasion. For as I look backward on December 11, 2012, I wrote: "When I closed out my last chapter of our first edition, of "Love Leaps Forward, Time Tilts Backward", my mother (Rosa Lee Napier Evans) very peacefully closed her eyes and entered into eternal rest. Now, interestingly enough, over a decade later, when I closed out the last chapter of the revision for the second edition, of our book, my husband closed his eyes and very peacefully entered into his eternal rest. Assuredly, life and death are in the hands of God.

Providentially, the day after my husband's death, I picked up our first edition of <u>"Love Leaps Forward, Time Tilts Backward"</u> and as I opened it, I was drawn to the "last words" of his foreword, (Rete…) *"I am blessed in knowing that our love will never end, but will one day transcend when we both meet our Lord face to face."* I became so excited, because after ten years, those *written words* became alive to me, and I was able to gain strength and comfort at the very time that I needed it most. That day, I felt my husband's love and his presence, as the glory of God filled the room. So, today, I say, with eternal love, "I now wait patiently, until that day when I meet our Lord face to face." ***Matthew 22:23-32***

DEDICATION
Doc and Grannie Goo

This book with its revision, is dedicated to the church of the living God, and to our wonderful children, grandchildren and great-grandchildren, as it relates to God, and "this generation" and end time revelation.

Behold, children are a heritage from the Lord,

The fruit of the womb is a reward.

Psalm 127:3

All your children shall be taught by the Lord, and great shall be the peace of your children.

In righteousness you shall be established... **Isaiah 54:13-14**

Revs' Antonio Donzaleigh Ezell, Sr. & (Crystal White) Ezell

Antonio Donzaleigh Ezell, Jr. (AsaYahu)/
Ashlee (Dixon) Ezell (Arukah)

(son) Rapha 'El Lavi Ezell

Alexis Donielle Ezell and daughter Aria Denise Ezell

Jacques Calvett Ezell (Tamyala Clarke) Ezell,
Kiya Odessa, Javian Calvier, Hadassah Abigail,
Jonathan Nehemiah, Joshua Judah Emanuel

Co-Pastor Vallena Vaselle Ezell (Pastor Dahl A.
Moss) Kahlil Idalis, Kyle Aaron Rashad

Jayda Simmons Moss/Kahlil Idalis,

Fredena Ozia Ezell (Kelvin Renaldo Hill)
Kelvyn Zimri Valece, Kye Horizon,

Kayen *"Freedom"* Ziare Hill *(Our Little Angel)*

*But if any widow, has children or grandchildren, let them first
learn to show piety at home and to repay their parents; for
this is good and acceptable before God.* **I Timothy 5:4**

*(It is my constant prayer that every widow, and any who may be
lost, destitute or poor and in need of help, that they will have the full
support of their children, grandchildren, family, friends and church.)*

And lastly, but not least, this book is dedicated to all the
many generations of parents, grandparents, and their families
in "this generation," and those to come. Also, to the many
servants of God, whose spouses have gone on before them
to become a part of God's assembly of that "great cloud of
witnesses", who bear record of our faith, while we who are yet
alive, continue to proclaim love, peace and joy in the Holy
Ghost, as we sing praises and testify to the goodness and grace
of our God through our Lord and Savior Jesus Christ.

*Jesus Christ Son of the living God is still alive and
well, on planet earth, even in the world today, working
signs, wonders, and miracles, through His Spirit.*

…I will declare Your name to My brethren;

And again:

"I will put my trust in Him."

And again:

Here am I and the children whom God has given Me."
Hebrews 2:13

"I will declare Your name to My brethren;

In the midst of the assembly I will sing praise to You."
Hebrews 2:12

Jesus Christ is the same yesterday, today and forever. **Hebrews 13: 8**

Jesus Christ Son of the living God is still alive and well, on planet earth, even in the world today, working signs, wonders, and miracles, through His Spiri!

Hallelujah! Hallelujah! Hallelujah!

All scriptures are taken from New King James Bible, unless otherwise indicated.

INTRODUCTION

At age sixty-three, I remembered that one of my childhood dreams was to write a book. However, since I loved poetry, I expected someday to write a book of inspiring poems. But now at age 74, after fifty-two years of marriage, I found myself writing my second edition *of "Love Leaps Forward, Time Tilts Backward" Until Death Do We Part,* which I now know was divinely inspired.

After much prayer and consideration, my husband and I set out on yet another journey of recalling, recording and updating some memorable events of our lives past and present with some changes and updates, while yet praying that others may be blessed from reading them. The experiences we shared and continued to share from our past and those we share even now, have greatly impacted our lives and now my future.

When I started this revision, my husband was sitting in the chair beside me, but now, as I finish the final touches, I sit beside an empty chair, as my husband is no longer with me. *But I am not alone.* I feel another presence strengthening me, as I recall the many memories of our accomplishments, and share the stories of sicknesses, pains, sorrows, and failures, and now, even *death.* I am thankful that we wrote these experiences together 10 years ago, because it is a lot harder for me to travel down memory lane today, than it was 10 years ago, while my husband walked with me.

Over the years, my husband and I shared many life experiences, but the most memorable events were centered upon our love for each other and eventually our love for God. Therefore, I dedicate this final edition with all my love to my late husband and the ONE true and living God, whom we both came to love and know. *1 Corinthians Chapter 13*

Though I always loved my husband, over the years I have learned that I must love the Lord my God with all my heart and with all my soul and all my mind *Deuteronomy 6:5*. I know some have said that we must have a love for God before we can truly love others. Well, this could be true, but I'm always doing things, backward. Sadly, I must admit that I loved my husband long before I came to truly know and love God, or at least I thought so. It was only after experiencing the many ups and downs of love and life that I came to know God through His Son Jesus Christ and learned to experience what God had in mind when He created us and love.

I really wish I had known God before I loved my husband. I am sure had I known and loved God first, our lives would have been much more fruitful and productive. I guess there is no reason to think backward, but I suppose we all do at one time or another. In my mind, everything just seems to tilt backward, except love. Love always seems to leap forward.

This brings me to the title and purpose of this book with its editions: Love leaps forward, Time tilts backward! Until Death Do We Part.

I wrote in our first edition that this narrative of our life story was specially written for that season. Well, it is even more so, now. As I began to reminisce and look over the years of our life together, I realized that times have changed even more so, and time seems to have really sped up. When I look back, I can remember when love was considered "a many splendored things." I remember "Callow Fellows" walking home from school carrying their favorite sweetheart's books. Ten years later, I can *still* remember a time when a date meant a quick trip to the ice cream parlor or a slow drag on the dance floor, and young girls would dream about someday becoming engaged and marrying that "special" guy. But, now, I don't think as many young girls spend hours daydreaming and sharing their thoughts with one another about becoming engaged hoping to someday marry that "special" guy. And 10 years later, after the national law was passed (June 26, 2015), marriage is no longer considered just between one man and one woman.

What happened? I don't know. Did we paint a false picture of what God intended marriage to be? Did husbands and wives somehow give love and marriage a bad name? Did we spend so much time focusing on the negatives that we failed to proclaim the positives? I think so. My husband and I repented because we too are guilty of mishandling one of God's most precious unions which He honored so much that He compared it to His church *Ephesians 5:25-26.* We were sorry for whatever role we played in diminishing God's ordained purpose for male and female as husbands and wife, but we are forever grateful that we have been redeemed by His love. For in spite of all of the heartaches, hardships, and mistakes we encountered in our marriage, we still believe that marriage between a man and a woman is one of God's most cherished possessions.

Therefore, I share this revised edition, as a testimony that love between a husband and a wife can still remain steadfast even in the worst of times. It is even written to those persons who might have become disillusioned after seeing so many couples give up and "throw in the towel." "Our story" is also written to inspire husbands and wives who may be struggling in their marriages. It is written for those couples who need to hear some encouraging words telling them to hang in there or that they can make it. This book is written to remind all of us that God does love and honor His ordained marriages.

We also want to acknowledge those who are single that you too are most valued in God's kingdom, as you develop and grow into a loving relationship with Him through His Son Jesus Christ. *I Corinthians 7:32* We declare and proclaim that no matter where you are in life, God is still involved in all of your life circumstances and His hand of lovingkindness, righteousness and judgment are ever present. *Jeremiah 9:24*

Finally, we offer a "Gift of Celebration and Praise" to those husbands and wives who never even thought of giving up, and also to those who have come to understand their purpose in their God-ordained union and make a daily and conscious effort to stay together. We celebrate those couples, who like us, continue to keep the words in mind, "until death do, we part."

We share this book of transparency with a hint of history and a trace of heritage which highlights stories of our past that embrace love and celebrates life as it was, as it is, as it comes, and as it goes. For even as time has the tendency to sometimes linger and tilt backward, love sometimes seems to speed up and take us by surprise. That is why I say, love leaps forward, but time tilts backward.

SECTION ONE

TIME TILTS BACKWARD

My Town

I grew up in a rural town in Middle Georgia known as Fort Valley. My home was nestled in a small neighborhood which one might call the "other side" of the tracks. The houses were different shapes, sizes, and colors and resembled a picture painted on the front of a puzzle box. They stood proudly in a long straight line on each side of the road from Front Street to Back Street. I never realized it until I got older, but the people who lived on Front Street had the larger homes and were actually the "Joneses." There was a certain indication of the distribution of wealth seen on Front Street that was not seen on the others. I lived somewhat in the middle of the neighborhood in an average-sized white house with black shutters. From the outside, it looked beautiful. The lawn was well manicured and on each corner of the yard were large forest green baskets my father had carved into different shapes: and a pole with a man's head made of concrete who was smoking a pipe and a bald eagle on a pole on the other side of the yard.

Of course, the outside was quite deceiving because once you were inside our home, you were faced with walls without paint, ceilings that dropped, and uncovered floors, all trademarks of my father who started the work and never completed it. The house was cold, damp, dark, and dingy on the inside, but I loved it all the same. But there was my Pomegranate Tree that seemed to redeem all of the unfinished projects of my father. The one he planted showed me how in one moment, the hands of a father could plant seeds in the earth which would last a lifetime for his children. Also, the people who lived in my neighborhood were wonderful. The neighborhood was filled with a blend of grandparents, parents, and children who were all just "common" folks living together in an area called "Griffin Line."

The streets were filled with laughter, and they were always crowded with children playing and horns blowing as parents screamed: "Get out of the road!" If you asked me, the weather was always perfect, no matter the time of year. Whether it was the hot and muggy summer or the far too-cold winters, I enjoyed them both. The weather during the spring and fall was likely the best for others, but summer was my favorite simply because school was out. Never mind the heat, all of the children would gather and have fun outside excited that there was no more school or homework. The streets became our skating rinks and our stages for talent shows, while the vacant lots became our baseball and football stadiums. Our backyards became our makeshift basketball courts, a pool of ice-cold water that trickled down from the local ice plant was our swimming pool, and a tall grassy hill at the railroad tracks was our sliding board. We all had loads of fun together. Life for me was very simple and unassuming. I never considered that we were poor and gave no thought to the rich. No matter what life held for me I was able to take it all in stride and enjoy it. I know now that God had placed something inside of me that was priceless and would carry me for the rest of my life. Beauty is what has already been created. This small town has never been so small that it denied my life from unfolding. This is where my story is told.

A Backward Glance

I t is hard for me to believe that I have actually lived for over six decades (seven, now). It seems like it was only yesterday I was outside playing with friends under my favorite tree. When I was young, I had quite a few friends but I always thought that I was somewhat shy., but my friends didn't think so. I was indeed secure in who I was. However, the enemy tries to confuse us and make us question who we are and whose we are. *Genesis 3:1* But as I traveled through life, somewhere along the way, I became secure in my thoughts *II Corinthians 10:5* and I came to realize that the way we feel about ourselves is somewhat directly related to understanding the plan that God has ordained over our lives. *Psalm 33:11* However, if the enemy had his way, I would have remained in a state of confusion. But somehow, through God's grace, I was always pushed forward, and I found that it was quite the opposite. From childhood to adulthood, God moved me in the direction He would have me to go. Like a river rushing and beating against the tides, God's power brought me to a place of wisdom, knowledge, and understanding. *Isaiah 11:1-2* Now I can *really* appreciate who I am and to *Whom* I truly belong. I know that life, death, and time are all in the hand of Almighty God and I have discovered that when God created each of us, He had a special plan for our lives. *Psalm 139:13-16*

Life for me really began when I was about nine years old and in the fourth grade. I cannot remember many significant events that took place in my life before then, but I clearly can recall two life changing events that stand out and have played a significant role in my life. One happened as I sat quietly in church one Sunday morning. I can remember sitting in church in the "Amen Corner" with my mother and younger sister. There was a row of elderly ladies sitting in their "special" corner on the right side of the church. They all wore big colorful hats with flowers and long feathers. Across from the women on the left-hand side was a row of six older men sitting on a very old rustic wooden pew. Underneath the pew were several wooden canes and worn hats. Since the pew did not have room for the men and all of their belongings, they kept their things under it. I looked at their faces and then I looked down at their shoes. Their faces looked as worn as their old shoes, but there was a certain glow about them. They seemed excited and overjoyed to be seated there.

As we sat quietly on our pews, an old man stood to his feet with a hymnal in his hands and walked slowly to the front of the church. His hair was frizzy and grey, and he wore an old tan, tattered jacket and a pair of faded brown trousers that looked much too large. As he stood before the congregation, he looked upward for a short while. I don't know if he was truly looking at something, of if he was just in deep thought. When I looked around, it seemed as though all eyes were on him. Eventually, however, he looked down at his hymnal and began singing an old familiar song: "Hold to God's Unchanging hand." His voice was weak and trembling, but his words were clear. The words that stood out most in my mind were: "Life is filled with swift transition. "He continued singing, "Naught of earth unmoved can stand. Build your hopes on things eternal. Hold to God's unchanging hand." He sang with a trembling voice as tears streamed down his face. It seemed as if his voice grew stronger and echoed throughout the church. Though I did not fully understand the full meaning of the words he sang, I had an idea the words meant that life was always changing and only God remained the same. ***Hebrews 13:8*** Without warning, he closed the book and began to dance as he sang his way back to his seat. I was incredibly moved by his singing and the dance that made him look as though he were leaping and jumping. I didn't know why, but my heart was also leaping with joy. I felt good inside.

After he sat down, a preacher, clothed in a long black robe, stood up and walked to the podium. He opened a large white Bible and began to read. He only talked for a short while and I cannot recall his message, only that it was unusually short for what I thought messages should be. After the preacher sat down, the choir stood up and sang a closing hymn: "Where He Leads Me, I Will Follow." I remember feeling very strange on the inside. It felt like butterflies were fluttering inside my stomach. Without thought or warning, something moved me and like the old man, I too jumped abruptly from my seat and began walking toward the preacher. My sister was sitting next to me, so she went with me. We stood before the preacher and he thanked us for coming up to join the church. What did we just do?

A few Sundays later, my sister and I were baptized. That morning, our mother gave us a change of clothes to carry with us. When we arrived at church and entered the sanctuary, I noticed the old wooden floor of the pulpit had been turned into a pool of water. Two ladies dressed in white walked over to us and led us into the back of the church. One of the ladies wrapped and pinned a white sheet around me and placed a white towel on my head. The other lady did the same to my sister. They told us this was a very special day in our lives because it was our Baptism Sunday. After they dressed us, they led us back into the sanctuary. Then the preacher said a few words to the congregation, called out our names and the ladies led us toward the pool of water. Afterwards the preacher led me to the water, leaned me back, and pinched my nose as he slowly lowered me into the water. Then he lifted me up. He did the same thing to my sister. Afterwards, the two ladies in white covered us with dry white sheets and led us to a room to help us change into our dry clothes. We were then taken back inside the church. We sat on the front pew and at the close of service, we received the "Right Hand of Fellowship" where the entire congregation welcomes you as a new member of the church family. The preacher shook our hand and welcomed us. This was also a very exciting time for my mother as she sat watching us with proud eyes. I was excited, but I did not realize that I had made a major transition into a new world of which I did not yet understand. It all happened so fast. Yes! Life is filled with "swift transitions." Though I didn't fully understand it then, this event was forever etched into my mind.

The next major event of my childhood happened at school when I was around ten years old. As I was sitting in an auditorium surrounded by teachers and students, I suddenly felt so alone. We were having our monthly assembly program and the auditorium was flooded by the sounds of excited children. Although it was very noisy, I managed to blot out all of the sounds and I began to do what I began to call "think backward". My mind drifted back to the evening my sister and I were baptized. After we came from church that Sunday, my parents had a very bad argument. For some odd reason, my father always became angry when we went to church. When we returned from church, as usual, he was drunk. I heard him in the bedroom swearing while my mother was screaming and crying. Apparently, my father showed my mother a gun, and rightfully so, she panicked and grabbed all of us, and headed for the door. There were six of us in all, but since my older brother, Wint, and sister, Cat, had already moved away, there were only four children living at home. My mother took us and ran next door to an old, vacant, and dilapidated house where we spent the night. The next day she found the owner and made arrangements for us to move in. At the time, I was too young to truly understand what was happening. I could not figure out why my mother felt like we were safer in an old abandoned home than in the place we had called home.

That evening, while my father was out drinking, we took a few clothes, personal items, and blankets and sneaked back into the old house. My father was on a binge so he never came to look for us. Since we didn't have any beds, we slept on the floor. I can recall that the house was very cold. Thank God for the heavy handmade quilts my grandmother had given us as family Christmas presents. They helped us make it through the long and cold nights. We stayed in the old house for about a week or so. Then, we finally moved in with my aunt and uncle who lived one street over. When they learned that we were staying in the old house, they moved all five of us in withtheir three children. They had five children of their own. I am sure it was not an easy decision to take us in. Lucille and Lola were away, but Rose, Christine, and Arthur, Jr. were still at home. It was a blessing to sleep in a warm bed again. I was very grateful and never forgot their kindness and generosity.

In the auditorium, I don't know how long I had been musing. I was so caught up in reminiscing that I was unaware of my surroundings and did not hear anything. That is until I was snatched back into reality by a booming voice shouting, "Give Me Liberty or Give Me Death!" I saw a little boy on stage with a voice as powerful as any adult I had ever heard. His voice was resounding and crisp. When I looked up, it seemed as if his eyes met mine and that he was only speaking to me. I found out later that he was reciting the words of an American orator and politician named Patrick Henry. After the young man finished his speech, I was mesmerized. I had a very strange feeling on the inside. It was different and somewhat unsettling. Those crazy little butterflies came back and they were fluttering even more, so than when I joined the church.

I never forgot that feeling and I never forgot the similar feeling I had as I walked down the aisle of the church that Sunday morning. The picture of the old man singing as he held on to his cane and the day of my baptism, as well as the picture of the young man standing on stage shouting the words of Patrick Henry never left me, even until this very day. These events were the beginning of a life long journey which I had not yet come to understand.

My Aunt and Uncle's Place

I remember life changed for me after those experiences. It seemed like those "swift transitions" continued from that day forward. During the year my aunt and uncle moved us in, there was a very cold winter. My uncle, cousin, and brothers had to cut down many trees and haul loads of wood to the house. There were several fireplaces throughout the house and my aunt and uncle always kept it nice and cozy. It was the month of December. In fact, it was almost Christmas! I had been waiting for Christmas all year because I loved Christmas time. I remember wondering how Christmas would be at my aunt and uncle's place. My past Christmases had always been wonderful. Christmas was usually the most enjoyable time of the year for my family. However, with my parents being separated, I was sure this year would be different.

Normally my father and mother bickered all the time, but at Christmas time, my mother and father actually seemed to get along. We would all get into a green panel truck and ride thirty miles to shop *(Sears and Roebuck)*. My father would buy several bags of candy and my mother would scold him about it. I guess she was embarrassed by how shamelessly and loudly he would eat all of our hard Christmas candy. Throughout the holiday season, my parents stored up nuts like squirrels. We always had walnuts, Brazil nuts, and hickory nuts. My father and mother also hid boxes of apples and oranges, raisins, and candy in the closets and underneath the beds. When we smelled the inviting scents all over the house, we knew then that Christmas was in the air! We had found most of our parents' hiding places, but we never touched anything. It was almost as though they were "sacredly preserved" until Christmas morning.

On Christmas Eve, while we were asleep, they would spread out a few clothes and toys. They would prepare each of us a shoebox of goodies. We could not wait to grab our personal shoebox with our names scribbled on it. Each child usually got a new pair of shoes on Christmas. When we saw the shoebox with our name on it, we not only knew we had goodies but a new pair of shoes. We were ecstatic! Can you believe we were excited just to get one new pair of shoes? Children today have rows of expensive name-brand shoes which they sometimes never wear. They somehow don't appear to be as grateful for the little things as we were. It could be that we give our children too much and too many choices. During my childhood days, I was excited just to get fruit and candy. We didn't have money to walk into a store and buy candy whenever we wanted. I remember, after a heavy rain, children would check the ditches near the drain pipes hoping to find a dime, nickel, or even a penny that the rain may have uncovered. If we found a coin, we would rush to the corner store to purchase a bar of candy or a pack of gum. One penny could buy a piece of candy. You could buy a pack of gum for five cents. I liked *Juicy Fruit*, because it was really sweet. My, how times have changed.

Christmas was always the most celebrated time of the year. All of the homes were decorated with strings of Christmas lights. The whole city was beautifully lit. I think there was even a wooden carved nativity scene on the courthouse lawn. On the morning of Christmas, we were always awakened by some crazy noise-filled toy. My father loved crazy mechanical toys. One year he bought us a dancing bear and a walking gorilla. He loved things that moved and made sounds. As I grew older, I realized that my father was a mechanical genius. He could make all kinds of things. He even made some of our Christmas gifts by hand. I thought my father could do anything. He was an electrician, farmer, carpenter, and taxidermist. He loved to hunt, fish, and stuff wild animals. He was a man of many talents whose alcoholism took control of his life. Sadly, he never used his talents to their maximum potential. That year, I felt sad because I knew I would miss him if he didn't spend Christmas with us.

We only stayed with our relatives for a short while. But for the life of me, I cannot remember that particular Christmas. I obviously blotted it out of my mind. That is the only Christmas I cannot recall. Somehow, all I can remember is my mother looking for a job and a place to move us. In time, she found several homes in which she could be a domestic worker, and we were able to move. Our relatives had been more than gracious to us, but it was overcrowded with ten of us in three bedrooms. Besides, my mother said that she did not want to "wear our welcome out". Neither did we. We all wanted to move into a house of our own.

My Aunt and Uncle's Place

(To Aunt Free and Uncle Jack)
Arthur Sr. and Freeman Ragin)

Some days when I'd get lonely
After my older siblings were gone
I'd get my little sister
And we'd visit my auntie's home.

My aunt would always welcome us
Somehow, we knew she cared.
She'd always have the table set
With delicious meals prepared.

My uncle also welcomed us
He'd pull us up a chair
And after we were seated
He'd lead us in a prayer.

My aunt and uncle had five kids
And it was hard to make ends meet.
But they never let that stop them
From asking us to eat.

There are so many other things
that they have done for me
That they deserve a "special" branch
Upon our family tree.

Retha Evans Ezell

Oh My: Where to Now?

My mother finally found us a place on the other side of town. My aunt and uncle drove us to our new place. I had hoped it would be close to our old neighborhood, but it wasn't. When my mother took us to our new place, I must admit that I was shocked. I knew that neighborhood. It was a run-down neighborhood known as the "Baptist Bottom." Baptist Bottom was the worst neighborhood known in town. Children would tease other children who lived in Baptist Bottom. I never teased children about where they lived, but I was sure I would become the laughing stock of my class when my friends found out I had moved there. I couldn't believe another house could be as bad as the old dilapidated house from which my aunt and uncle moved us. But believe me, this one was worse. This place was much smaller, the floors had holes in them and one room had no floors at all. I had heard in Sunday School that Jesus walked on water and when it rained so did, we.

Our mother told us that this was going to be our new home and it would be great. That evening, she went to the store and bought groceries for a new recipe for us. She cooked and cleaned for a woman named "Miss Betty" who had shown her how to make Spanish Pork Chops. The pork chops were simmered in vinegar, smothered in tomato sauce, and covered with a layer of sautéed onions. My mother let me use the new electric can opener Miss Betty had given her. We had never had an electric can opener so I was excited. I remember using it to open a can of green peas. I don't know why, but back then we called them "English peas." We also had buttered brown and serve rolls, mashed potatoes, and ice-cold lemonade. It's funny that I can still recall that meal and almost taste it just as if it were yesterday. I guess I felt my mother's pain and her love as she tried to make us feel better. I think this special meal was her way of saying, "It's not as bad as it looks." This worked. The meal was delicious and for a moment, I almost forgot about my father's absence and the rundown house with dirt for floors in one of the rooms.

After about three months, we moved again. My mother told us our new place would be much better and girls our own age lived next door. Full of anticipation, I took my best friend and classmate to share in my excitement. I was glad to show off my new place. I was happy to move almost anywhere. Who wouldn't be glad to move from Baptist Bottom? The new place was in walking distance from my school. We looked at the address I had scribbled on a piece of paper and started on our excursion to find my new home. We walked and walked. In my excitement, it seemed as if this walk lasted forever but the reality was that the house was only at the end of the road. When we finally arrived, we discovered the house looked as if it was in the road. Simply put, there was no front yard. I had never seen a house so close to the road, nor had I seen a house that had no front yard. At our old home, we always enjoyed playing in the front yard. As if that wasn't enough, when we walked toward the porch, a car skidded by and almost hit us. There was a long porch with two outside doors on opposite ends with several ladies sitting on it. There was also a large old tree in the yard with limbs that hung over into the street and underneath the tree were quite a few men playing checkers.

It was my first time seeing a Mulberry tree, and it was full of the largest blackberries I had ever seen. I ate some, and they were absolutely delicious. I thought mulberries grew on bushes like blackberries. I guess I thought this because we used to sing a song at school called: "Here We Go 'Round the Mulberry Bush" during our school devotion. I loved that song. It was an action song. It taught us early morning discipline. We learned we should wash our face, comb our hair, and brush our teeth every morning. It was fun to hear all of the children stomping their feet and marching around the classroom as if they were headed to school. Standing at the tree reminded me of how much I enjoyed school. Once again, my mind left where I was and traveled to another place.

As a young girl, I went to the local public school. In our current society, children no longer have the privilege of participating in early morning devotion at public schools. When I was in elementary school, we had devotion every morning. A devotion leader would be chosen by the teacher. It was a treat to be chosen as the devotion leader. Once chosen, the devotion leader stood in front of the whole class and we all sang, "Good morning, good morning, good morning to you. Bright sunshine, bright sunshine, oh, how do you do? We're all in our places with sunshiny faces, good morning to you." Then we all repeated the Pledge of Allegiance, sang the national anthem and "God Bless America." Our last song was. always, "America: My Country Tis of Thee." I remember for years I thought we were singing my country "tears" of thee. How fitting is this for today since we have moved so far away from our God and our protector? "My country 'tears' of Thee." I pray for the peace of Jerusalem *Psalm 122,* and many times, I do weep for America. *Psalm 9:20*

Also, during early morning devotion we had to recite a Bible verse. I remember the children who didn't know very many scriptures always said, "Jesus wept!" Can you believe we did all of this in fifteen minutes? We did so much in such a short time. We learned to greet each other with Good Morning songs that always put us in a joyful mood. Then we learned to acknowledge our Creator and our nation in those few minutes. We closed our devotion by saying the Lord's Prayer in unison.

Unfortunately, there are state and federal laws that forbid prayer in school now. Who would have thought? Well, times change, people change, and so do laws, and not always for the better. *Daniel 7:25* But we still have hope. That's how I felt about the place where we were moving. It was a change. Even though, it was no house of luxury, I still had hope that one day we would move back home or to a much better place.

Once we got settled in our new place, I learned that the house we lived in shared space with another family. Well, that explains the two doors. The bathroom, back porch, front porch and yard (such as it was) were called common areas. We shared everything except our one bedroom and the kitchen. The bathroom was on the back porch. I hated going outside every morning waiting in line to use the bathroom. My mother always gave us bleach to wipe the toilet seat. She told us this would help to fight off germs, since so many of us were using the toilet. But all in all, our neighbors were rather nice and I enjoyed playing with kids my own age. There were six children who ranged in all ages. Their family was even more crowded than we were. They had eight people living in their small place.

By then, my brother Wint had also come back home to live with us while my second eldest brother who we nicknamed "Hot Chow" went off to service. His real name was Alfonzo. So, my mother, Wint (Winfred), youngest brother "Hud" (Hudman), youngest sister Trisha (Patricia) and I all lived together in that crowded space. It became very uncomfortable at times, but we made it. Wint had returned home to find work and had been home for several months. He was a construction worker and his job in the city had ended. Once he returned home, he found a job laying cement blocks on a church renovation project. The job was outside work and the weather was changing. I remember it was a very a cold winter, that year, but my brother didn't seem to mind. Of course, at this particular time, it was his best choice.

Not only was it cold, but it was almost Christmas again. It seemed as though we were always in transition during the Christmas season. I read a story once about the "Grinch who stole Christmas." Was the old "Grinch" on a private mission to steal my Christmas joy? Well, if so, he didn't. My two older brothers made sure we had a very nice Christmas that year. They knew my mother had very little income, so with the little money he had, Wint bought my sister and me a little pink toaster, a blender and a toy sewing machine. Much to our surprise, we also received a box from my brother "Hot Chow" who was in the military. He sent us each beautifully embroidered sweaters and pretty gold butterfly pendants. When we opened the butterfly's wings, a watch was inside. We were amazed. He also included nice gifts for my mother and my brothers. In spite of our circumstances, and unlike the year before, I was able to remember every detail.

A few months later, my mother told us we would be moving again. "*Oh My!*" I thought. "*Where to now?*" Much to my surprise, my mother told us we were moving back to our old home. Though I wished it would happen, I had not expected it would happen so quickly. I could not understand why we would be moving back home, especially since my parents were separated. Were they getting back together? My mother didn't give us much information, but I was sure that later on, she would tell us more.

Life Without Father

I was sure my mother would give us more information about the move, and she did. This time, she really gave us some good news. Our lives would be changing again, but this time for the better. My mother told us that she and my father were in completion of their divorce proceedings. I knew they had separated, but I didn't know about the divorce. My father had been living in the home while we moved from place to place. The judge had ordered him to give us back our old home. The judge also ordered him to pay each minor child twenty dollars per week for child support. Wow! Twenty dollars sounded like one hundred to me. Of course, my father never paid the money every week. He would pay one week and skip the next. He was paid bi-weekly, so instead of giving us twenty dollars per week, he gave us twenty dollars every other week. During those days, there was no real legal recourse for child support, The child support collection system was not set up until 1975 under President Gerald Ford, and overhauled by President Bill Clinton in 1996. Therefore, back then, we just took whatever he gave us and were grateful. At any rate, it was more than he had given us in the past.

I was thankful my parents were not reuniting. Though my parent's separation had caused some major changes and adjustments in our lives. I was thankful I was no longer awakened in the middle of the night by terrible arguments and even physical fighting. I never dwelt on my parent's separation. By the grace of God, I was never angry with my parents after they separated. However, I did get in a terrible argument with my father, one night while in a crowd, he made some derogatory remarks about my mother. Still, I never really blamed them for the things that took place in their marriage. But I did wonder why they could not stay together. Of course, as I got older,

I knew my father's drinking played a major role in causing friction within the relationship. Over the years, I also learned that alcohol is one of the leading problems attributed to destroying families and breaking up homes. I am sure there were other issues which led to their separation. Whatever the reason, I knew we would have to go on with our lives without a father. Though I was only about eleven years old at the time, I somehow knew it would be different.

Once the divorce was final, some years, later, my father remarried. He moved a few streets over from us. His new wife had four children of her own. He moved on with his life and so did we. My mother continued her role as head of our household and did quite well. I can remember seeing her walk from the store with an armload of groceries. She had an account at the local grocery store. Many times, she brought a few groceries from the market near her job. As a domestic worker, she traveled over sixty miles per day to make a few dollars. She would be very tired at the end of the day. She would repeat her favorite Psalm aloud most nights (Psalm 121), especially when she was having struggles. We all tried to help her as much as possible. Trisha and I shared in the household chores while Hud considered himself to be the "Head Chef." For several years, he cooked us some very good meals. In his later years, this cooking experience landed him a summer job as a short order cook at one of the major hotel chains in Atlanta. We all shared in the household responsibilities and learned to adjust as best we could without a father in the home.

We did not see very much of our father after he moved. As I grew older, I mainly only remember visiting him about our financial support. By then, he was remarried. His new wife was always very kind to us. In addition to her own four children, she and my father had one child. Our sister was named Wylene. Though we lived close by, my father never tried to bring us together. Under the circumstances, I guess he didn't know how. We only shared a few brief visits. When I did visit my father's home, I really felt sorry for the children in the house. Isn't that funny? I felt sorry for them. Whenever I visited their home, my father was sitting in a chair, drinking, and spewing profanity. He scolded them, and I did not miss those days.

Occasionally, my father would bring the child support to us. He would pull up outside and blow the horn, and we would run out to get the check. That was the extent of our relationship. However, I can also recall the special times he would stop by our house with fruit and vegetables on his truck. In addition to his regular job, he was a farmer. He traveled through our neighborhood selling produce. His father (Grin daddy Frank). We called him this because he always had a big "*grin*" whenever he saw us. He was known as one of the best farmers in the region and my father was known as a "chip off the old block." His mother (Ma Minnie) also farmed and was an excellent gardener. Every year, she had a beautiful flower garden with zinnias, roses, and lilies. But my father enjoyed raising fruit and vegetables. Most of all, he enjoyed raising his prized watermelons.

Some months after we moved back home, he stopped by and gave us one of his prize watermelons. Maybe it was his way of saying, "I 'm glad you have the house back." Later that evening, we had a watermelon party with our old friends. After we finished eating our watermelon, we went outside to find bottles to make a bottle doll. We loved to make bottle dolls. We would find a pop bottle, packaging rope, and newspaper to make our doll. First, we used the bottle for the body of the doll. Next, we put a rubber band around the end of the rope and placed the rope inside the neck of the bottle. Then, we untwisted the rope and it would hang down like long strands of hair. Finally, we would make clothes for our doll from the newspaper. Voila! We had a beautiful fully dressed American doll. No one would ever know it was just a bottle. We always tried to jump rope with the long left-over pieces. Once we finished playing with our dolls, we went back inside for more watermelon. I can remember that day so well. We planted the seeds in little jars, hoping to yield us a crop one day. We also played games spitting seeds at one another. The watermelon was sweet and so was life. It was a wonderful home coming celebration.

The older neighbors also had fun. They too were thankful we had moved back into our home. My mother loved to visit the older women in the neighborhood. Whenever anyone would get sick in the neighborhood, she would go and assist them without charge. My mother always wanted to be a nurse. However, her father would not let her finish high school. She had to work in the fields to help earn money for the household. As a result, she insisted that all of her children finished high school and received a good education. She would always encourage us to do our very best in spite of the many challenges of life. Her words of wisdom and sound advice have been inspirational throughout my life. I knew she really regretted not finishing high school. I suppose later on this had a lot to do with me always trying to do my best in school. She was very pleased many years later when I was awarded the Joseph B Whitehead. I showed her my mentor *Joseph B. Whitehead Coca-Cola Scholars' Education of Distinction Award* and gifts (2004-*NeKeisha Randall,* Coca-Scholar Foundation Scholar.)

After moving back home, thoughts of my father weighed heavily upon me. My father was different. At the age of eleven, I should have known him, but I didn't. I guess it was because we never spent much quality time together. Even though I never really knew him, I had mixed emotions about his leaving. In some ways, I missed not having a father in the house, but I was thankful that we could now have peace in our home. Though these were not the best of times, I was excited about our new life in our old home but my excitement did not last very long.

Shortly after we moved back home, I was awakened one night by screams and banging on the wall. The sounds were coming from my mother's room. I stood outside the door for a minute. When I opened the door, I saw broken tables and chairs scattered all over the room. My mother was shouting and screaming obscenities. She had a wooden coffee table raised high above her head. I started screaming, "Mae Dear! Mae Dear!" which is what we called our mother. Other children in our neighborhood called their mothers *Ma Dear, Muh Dear* or *Madea.* I guess they were all derivatives of "Mother Dear." As I ran toward my mother, I saw her pick up her favorite lamp and whirl it across the room. It was then that I knew we were in trouble, so I ran out of the room and closed the door.

By this time, my brother and sister had awakened. They were in the next room. We all got dressed as quickly as possible and ran to our aunt and uncle's house. My heart was racing and I was almost panting as we pounded on their door in the middle of the night. My uncle finally opened the door. When we explained what happened, he immediately called the police, and for the life of me, I could not understand why.

My uncle and aunt got dressed hurriedly and we all rushed back to our house. By the time we arrived, two police officers were getting out of their car and my uncle took them inside. The two men came out tussling with my mother. They were having a difficult time getting her to the car. One would think that two adult men could easily handle one small woman, but they couldn't. They finally got my mother to the car and sat her in the back seat. I had never been that close to a police car. They strapped my mother down and handcuffed her as though she were a criminal. I was frightened. Once the officers had my mother settled, they began conversing with my uncle. Afterwards, they got into their car and left with my mother in the back seat. Where were they taking her? My aunt and uncle had us to gather some clothes so we could stay with them. Once I got in bed, it took a while for me to get to sleep.

I was awakened the next morning by the smell of cinnamon toast, oatmeal, and hot chocolate. My aunt always cooked a wholesome and hearty breakfast. She had said many times that breakfast was the most important meal of the day. After we finished eating, my aunt told us she had called Cat and Wint. He had recently returned to Atlanta after his local construction job ended in town to live with my sister and her family. They would be coming to my aunt's house that afternoon. After the scare of the night before, I was happy they were coming and could not wait for them to arrive.

My Father and I

(To Daddy, Young Calvin Evans)

My father left home when I was nine
Leaving me many memories behind.
Though not all pleasant they were a part of life
Portraying a story of husband and wife.

A story of two people who no longer could share
The snares of life we sometimes must bear.
It's sad but it's happening even today
When two people's love seems to fade away.

Sometimes, they have children who are caught in a bind
A new way of adjusting to life they must find.
I found my strength within a tree.
A very lovely Pomegranate tree
A tree which my father planted for me.
It became my refuge, my shelter, my friend
It gave my life substance throughout and within.

My father never knew how much my tree meant
He was never aware of the hours I spent.
Sitting, thinking, and planning my life
Warding off fears, disappointments and strife.

Sometimes, I 'd think he had done nothing for me
But then I'd begin to remember my tree.
Which healed me when I was sick one time

LOVE LEAPS FORWARD

When around it the catnip and garlic were found.

I'd think of the day I would have failed my test
But I spelled "pomegranate" and was the best.
Though my father wasn't there for me every day,
He left me something to help guide my way.
In a way, he helped me with growing pains
He too helped make me the girl I became.

Retha Evans Ezell

There's No Place Like Home

Wint managed to get off work early, so he and Cat were waiting for us at our aunt's house when we came home from school. My brother was always moving from one place to the next trying to find work. Whenever one construction was finished, he would relocate. He usually traveled from our small rural town to Atlanta. That particular time he had gotten a better job with the Atlanta Police department. During the early 60's and 70's, many young people were moving from rural areas to Atlanta. My older sister and her husband had lived there for years. I was happy all of them were coming to check on us. After we ate dinner, they discussed the incident with us. They wanted to let us know that our mother had a nervous breakdown. The policemen had taken her to a mental institution about fifty miles away. I didn't fully understand. What could cause a mother to be sitting calmly in the living room with her children earlier in the day and then later that night loses all control?

Since we were all in school, my brother and sister suggested it would be best for us to move in with our aunt and uncle to which they quickly agreed. They explained things to us as best as they could. My aunt had tears in her eyes, and I'm sure she felt her sister's pain in every situation. She told us our mother had mental health issues that we never knew about. I sat there amazed as she recounted my mother's story. My mother had lost two sons. I learned that I had two other brothers I knew nothing about. First, there was Alvin who was two years old when he died of pneumonia. Then, a few months later, Calvin, who was only about six months old, died of smoke inhalation. We were told one particular night my father had not returned home, so my mother rushed out to buy some milk. The store was only a block away, but while my mother was gone, Wint was playing with matches and set the house on fire. They told us he and my sister hid under the house and someone from the crowd pulled them out of the fire. However, no one knew the baby was left inside. Calvin was consumed by the fire, and my mother could never forget that terrible day. She had not even had time to fully mourn the death of Alvin before she faced another tragedy. I don't know how this accident affected my father. Maybe losing two sons so close together contributed to his drinking problem.

We were told these back-to-back tragedies caused my mother to be very fragile and damaged her mentally. Afterwards, she was in a very serious state of depression. I am sure fathers are affected by the death of a child, but I imagine it is even more devastating for a mother. Since the mother carries the baby, the child becomes a part of her. For a mother, losing a child is like losing a part of herself.

After hearing about my mother's past, I had a better understanding then and even now of what happened the night of her nervous breakdown. I could see how memories of these terrible tragedies could haunt her and cause her to become seriously depressed. Watching my mother, I saw the way separation, divorce, and being a single mother affected her. This, coupled with the loss of her sons, was too much for my mother to withstand. It was heartbreaking, and I wished I could have found some way to help her. Over the years, my mother's mental health declined. There was not much we could do except offer our love and support.

The truth of this matter is that my mother never healed mentally or emotionally. It was difficult for her to forgive my father or herself for the life crises they experienced over the years of their marriage. She still had those scars even now at age 94. Even in a state of what physicians *called* dementia, my mother muttered and sometimes ranted and raved about my father. She still talked about the two sweet little boys. She spoke of them as if they are still with her. She went to a mental institution, but her mental health was always unstable. She had good and bad days. As I recall, there were sometimes months, and other times years, between her relapses, so she spent most of her adult life in and out of mental institutions.

I vividly remember my first visit to the mental institution. When we walked in, my mother did not seem to even know who we were. She just sat and murmured muffled phrases, arguing with my father as if he were sitting next to her. It was difficult seeing her that way, but at least we had the opportunity to visit her. We all hugged her, but I don't think she even knew we were there. I had a sad feeling of emptiness in my heart and a lump in my throat as we rode away and saw the white gated fence close behind us. One gate opened to let us in and another gate closed to shut us out. Isn't that just how life is? One gate opens and another gate closes and it is up to us to determine what we will do after we transition to the other side.

When we arrived back home with our aunt and uncle, there was not much to do other than read. I read a lot at my aunt's house. There were always magazines spread out on a shiny coffee table. I really enjoyed reading because it allowed me to escape into another world. It also increased my vocabulary. I loved looking up the words each month in the Reader's Digest "Word Power." I think reading helped me a lot in school. When I really think about it, my aunt and uncle's family was somewhat different. Her children *actually* called her, "Mother Dear". They did not have a lot, but they always seemed to have enough for themselves and others. Like clockwork, they ate three meals a day. The entire family sat at the table together, and my uncle always said grace. We were all blessed to eat meals around their table, and I was very grateful for their hospitality. Even still, I really missed my mother and longed to go back home. There's no place like home.

Illustrated by: Lola Ragin Morrow

My Mother Wasn't

First prize, Fort Valley Leader Tribune Mother's Day
(Peach County Chamber of Commerce)
(To Mae Dear, Rosa Lee Napier Evans)

My mother wasn't always as happy as a lark
There were some times that I recall
Her days were rather dark.
My mother didn't always get me the things I wanted
There were some things I thought I would get, but I was disappointed.

My mother wasn't always there to do the household chores,
So, I learned how to cook and clean
And wash and iron my clothes.
She never stayed at home all day to cook me fancy meals
Instead, she had to work you see, to help pay all the bills.

Now some may find it very hard to truly understand
Why I still think my mother is the best in all the land.
But there's one thing I failed to say in all the things above,
No matter what the case may be,
She always showed me love.

Retha Evans Ezell

Section Two

Time To Make Friends

"A friend loves at all times." **Proverbs 17:17**

Peanuts (Trisha)! Popcorn (Emma) and Cracker Jacks! (Rete)

The time came for my mother to be dismissed from the mental institution. I was happy to hear that she was coming home. My aunt told us that my mother was going to move to the city with my older sister because our sister wanted her to have a change of scenery. I had hoped we would all move back home, but by then, I was old enough to understand. I knew my sister wanted to do what was best for our mother. My mother also talked to us about the move. At first, I was excited because I thought a change of scenery would be good for all of us, but my excitement once again was short-lived when my mother told me I would not be moving with them to Atlanta. Surprisingly, she told me she was only taking my younger sister with her and I would have to continue living with my aunt and uncle. I could not believe she would do that especially since my sister and I were very close. We were like two peas in a pod. Though I was eleven years old and had learned a lot about life over the years, that one really caught me off guard. I was disappointed and devastated.

My mother took my younger sister in the back room and she began to pack. Once they finished packing, they got into the car ready to leave. Hiding the tears in my eyes, I quickly said goodbye to my mother and sisters and headed to sit on the front porch. I wanted to get my mind onto other things. The sun had set, it was a beautiful night, and the sky was filled with stars. I loved to gaze at the stars. I was always looking for the Big Dipper and the Milky Way.

From a distance, I heard a loud voice. The voice was strong and seemed to echo through the night. As I looked down the road to see where it was coming from, I saw a young man with an old washing machine agitator shaped like a megaphone. Like a vendor selling goods, he cried out, "Peanuts, Popcorn and Cracker Jacks. Get ' em while they're hot!" I felt as if the voice was calling me. It was very distinct and familiar, so I went to the side of the road. It was none other than the orator who I'd named, "Little Patrick Henry." He and his friends, *Corn Truck (Bobby) and Curtis,* were gathered under the streetlight. They all lived several streets behind us, and I had not seen them since I had moved in with my aunt. I watched excitedly as he left his friends and began running toward my aunt's house.

A few months before that night, my sister and I were going to visit my girlfriend, Margie, who had lived on back street. That particular day, we were walking through a path that joined our streets together. The path was very narrow, so being the gentlemen he was, Little Patrick Henry had moved over to let us pass. I will always remember his words, "After you ladies." And now here was that voice again and those same butterflies found their way back home, right in the middle of my stomach.

I had never seen him out at night. He started walking in my direction, and I was surprised when he turned into my yard. He said hello and started talking and asking me questions. He asked about my sister. Obviously, he had watched us long enough to know we were inseparable. As we talked, he also asked me about my friend next door. He told me later that he had watched us for a while and saw us as three young girls stuck together in a box of Cracker Jacks. So, he gave us the nickname of *Peanut, Popcorn* and *Cracker Jacks.* My little sister was Peanut, our neighbor Emma was Popcorn, and I was Cracker Jacks. I told him that I had nicknamed him "Patrick Henry."

It's ironic that he named us Peanut, Popcorn, and Cracker Jacks. Before my parent's separation, my father would bring home boxes of Cracker Jacks as our bi-weekly treat. A box of Cracker Jacks meant it was payday. That was one of the positive things I remember sharing with my father. I really did love those Cracker Jacks, but I especially loved the prizes inside. One of my favorites was the magnifying glass.

My sister Trisha and I, would take the magnifying glass, stand in the sun, and place the glass over our wrists. The glass would get so hot that our wrists would burn. This became one of our favorite childhood games. Sometimes, we would find a *ring* in the box. I was excited about the nickname "Cracker Jacks" that my new found friend had given me. I liked it much better than the name "Slim" which my brother Al and his friends called me.

As we sat and talked, I began to tell him about my sister and mother moving to Atlanta. He thought I was just visiting my aunt that night and didn't know that was my new home. I told him I did not know how long they would be away and I began to share my feelings with him. I could not imagine why I was telling him all of this, but without thinking, I shared how hurt I truly was. All the questions I wanted answers to came out of my mouth that night. Why *did* my mother not take me with her? Why would she separate me and my little sister? Why was I the one she left behind? She should have known I wanted to stay in the city, too. Though my mother had left my younger brother, also I still missed my sister. Before "Little Patrick Henry" left, he told me not to worry and assured me everything would work out and that my mother and sister would be back home before I knew it. I could tell he was really concerned.

Suddenly, without warning, he changed the subject. This was another moment of a "swift transition." He began talking about school and fine arts and after a while, I had almost forgotten the shambles my life was in at that time. For a moment, I forgot about my sister and mother being away and enjoyed the conversation. In the background, I heard my aunt calling my name. It was getting late. As I said goodnight, I experienced the same feeling I had in the fourth grade while sitting in the noisy auditorium. But this time, though it was still an unsettling feeling, I felt good inside, as if I had reunited with a friend I had known for years. I enjoyed talking with him and wished he could stay longer. I did not want to say goodnight, but I did. I smiled as I recalled my mother's words: "All good things must come to an end." I waved goodbye and watched as he raced toward the light down the street to join his friends. He shouted back, "Hope to see you again!" Me, too, I thought. I felt good as I watched the shadows of him and his friends in the dark, but as soon as I went inside and closed the door, the sadness returned. I felt very much alone. My thoughts returned to my mother and sister, and I wondered when or if they would come back home.

My mother and Trisha stayed in Atlanta for a full year. My aunt and her family were very kind to me, so I made it through this difficult time. When the day finally came for my mother and sister to come home, my older sister came with them. Unbeknownst to me, she was preparing to move back to finish her education at the local college. She had gotten married before she finished college and had started a family of her own. I was excited when I heard the news and looked forward to all of us moving back to our old home. However, she didn't move back right away.

When I returned home, the first thing I did was sit in my favorite spot. I sat on the front porch admiring the beautiful pomegranate tree my father had planted years before. I always loved that tree. I loved to see the beautiful orange blossoms peeping through the crisp green leaves. I enjoyed sitting and watching them change into beautiful orange bulbs, crowned in all of God's glory. The *pomegranate* is a very unusual fruit. The outside skin is very tough. It also has very thin coverings that hide the plump red seeds. The covering is bitter, but the seeds are sweet and juicy. When I think about the pomegranate, it is a lot like life. Sometimes life can be tough and hard to understand, but if you just keep tugging at it and remove the skin and bitter covering, you will be amazed at what is on the inside. And though life has its moments of bitterness, underneath it all is a certain sweetness. The day that my mother and sisters returned, I felt that sweetness of life. It finally felt like things would return to normal, whatever normal was for us by then. I could once again enjoy the company of my next-door neighbor. I could not wait to tell my new friend that "Peanut, Popcorn and Cracker Jacks" were back together again, but I had not seen him since that night. School was out, so I had not even gotten a glimpse of him.

A few weeks after we moved back home, I looked across the street, and there he was. He was visiting my new neighbors. My girlfriend Margie had moved across the street, and they were sitting on the porch together. They were laughing and playing a game. When I saw them sitting together, I felt very uncomfortable, but I didn't exactly know why. As I looked up again, Margie was waving her hand and inviting me over to play with them. When I walked over, they were playing a game with dried peach seeds. We had lots of peaches in our area, hence the name, "Peach County."

The name of the game was "Jackstones", and I did not know how to play, but Little Patrick Henry quickly taught me the game. After all, according to him, he was the "Jackstone Champion." He took 10 of the seeds in his hand and threw them up in the air. He turned his hand over and caught one seed. He then began to throw up one seed as he tried to pick up the other seeds that were left. He did it. I guess he was the champion. Finally, I tried it, but it took me a while to get the hang of it. Eventually, I finally became good at it. We all played and had fun together. At the close of the evening, as darkness shadowed the clouds, we played another game called, "Spin the Bottle". Several other kids had joined us, and we all took turns spinning a soda pop bottle. If the neck of the bottle fell on someone of the same sex, you would spin again. If it fell on someone of the opposite sex, you would give that person a smack on the cheek. I had no idea that we were being taught a very fundamental principle of God's plan of creation for his family. Maybe a simple game of "Spin the Bottle" could put a picture in the mind of our children today that God created male and female to become husband and wife. Children are so confused today about their gender, relationships, and marriage. It is even more difficult for them to make choices today, after 10 years have passed and we have new laws and societal changes. I never look down on anyone who chooses another way in any area of life, but I do feel compassion and wish that I could help them to see what I have come to know, as a more excellent way through Christ Jesus.

As we continued to play "Spin the Bottle", Little Patrick Henry began to take his turn and I secretly hoped his bottleneck would point toward me. But it didn't. Maybe next time! Nevertheless, we all had fun and it was an enjoyable evening. When we finished the game, he walked me to the edge of the yard. He was such a gentleman. As he said goodbye again, there was this peculiar feeling in the pit of my stomach. This time, the feeling was more intense than it was when I sat in the school auditorium and even when he sat with me on my aunt's front porch. Something was happening to me on the inside that I could not explain. There were the same butterflies inside of my stomach, but this time they seemed to have invited friends who were all dancing. What could it be?

The Letter

After my girlfriend moved across the street, I saw my friend quite often. He and Margie's brother (Corn Truck) were best friends. By the end of the summer, we all had become very close friends. The guys all spent hours playing under the streetlights while the girls sat on the front porch talking. Once the boys finished playing their games, we all sat on Margie's porch and played games together. I began to notice that when I would leave so would Little Patrick Henry. He would walk me across the street where we would talk for a few minutes and then head back over to Margie's with the other guys. Of course, during this time, girls had to be inside before the boys. One day Margie asked me if I knew Calvin, who I knew as "Little Patrick Henry," was her boyfriend. I only responded that I noticed they were a bit playful with each other. I had never really thought boyfriends or girlfriends but just friends. She told me she had known him when they lived on the street behind me. I didn't think much of it. I was just excited having such a wonderful time that summer. The summer had gone by much too fast and school would be here before we knew it.

By the time school started, Little Patrick Henry and I had become even closer friends. Once school began, we both signed up for drama club. Up until that year, I had hardly ever seen him at school. Maybe it was because I was not looking for him. Once school started, I saw him all the time. During our conversations over the summer, I discovered we both loved music, dancing, and public speaking. We found that we had a lot in common. Our teachers began to have us represent our school in all of the major fine arts festivals across the state and region. He was known for his captivating rendition of, "The Creation" from James Weldon Johson's book, God's Trombones.

We both usually won first place and received many trophies and awards for our school. We were a team. But most of all, we had the opportunity to ride the bus and spend time together without my girlfriend Margie. However, I was somewhat bothered by this. Was I being unfaithful to my friend? After all, she had already told me he was her very first boyfriend.

It is funny as we grow older, we learn to justify. It didn't take long for me to convince myself my relationship with Calvin was harmless. Since I had noticed she had other fellows who came over to visit her, I convinced myself it was okay for him and me to spend more time together. One day, not knowing how to handle the situation, I decided to ask her about the other guys. She answered me very nonchalantly that it was no big deal, and I was too young to understand. She told me that maybe one day I would. I felt belittled when she talked as if I was just a child, especially when she was only two years older than me.

But the truth was although we were close in age, she was much more mature. She always seemed to be in control and had so much confidence. She practically ruled her house in the evenings and at night. Sometimes, her mother and father worked night shifts. On those nights, she was the "Lady of the House." I had learned to do some things at home but nothing compared to all of the responsibilities Margie had. She had six younger siblings and could take care of a house better than most adults. She cooked, cleaned, ironed, and braided all of her little sisters' hair. Most mornings, she even dressed them for school. I thought she made the best fried chicken and fries in the world, and I will never forget the first time I watched her cut up a chicken. It was unbelievable how quickly and perfectly she divided it into eight pieces. She even took the time to teach me.

She was also full of wisdom, and I always wondered how she knew so much at such a young age. Many other young girls and guys in the neighborhood enjoyed just being in her company. Almost every evening, we all rallied around her on the front porch. She had become my best girlfriend and my confidante. I could share almost any secret with her except one! But soon, this one would be revealed.

One afternoon as we walked home from school, Calvin asked me to write him a letter. "A letter?" I asked. "Yes," he said, "Tell me how you feel about me." It was an unusual request from a friend, but I did it. And wouldn't you know it, that evening the letter dropped out of my pocket and Margie found it. I tried to grab it, but she picked it up and ran. She began to read it aloud. She stuffed it in her bosom. That night when he came over, she called me across the street and gave the letter to him. "Here's your letter I read, but it's okay, I have other guys." I could not believe she told him that. He did not say anything. He just took the letter and walked away. I left very embarrassed and confused. I did not want to see either of them the next day. The thought of facing them the next morning troubled me all through the night.

The next day, I saw Margie and she began to talk as if the incident had never happened. She was amazing. I had worried all night for no reason. To her, it was not that serious. But I still had to face Calvin. What would I say to him? Better yet, what would he say to me? I could not imagine how this situation would end. Surprisingly, after school, he did not say anything. He just took all of my books, placed them under his arm, and carried them for me for the very first time. We had walked home many times together, but this was the first time he had carried my books. I guess this meant we were a couple which made me feel really special.

Love Is in the Air

Now that our "little secret" was out, it seemed as though our relationship experienced one of those "swift transitions." We didn't play as much anymore with the other kids; instead, we spent most of our time together. We not only spent time together at home, but at school as well. Once we got home and finished our homework and chores, we would walk and sometimes ride our bikes around the neighborhood. We had really become a couple. I enjoyed talking with him. He was a very good listener, and he had a great sense of humor. We shared a lot of wonderful times together and helped each other through many of the trials of becoming "teenagers." Time was moving quickly. Margie was now seventeen and hanging out with older guys. As she grew older, she had less time to spend with me, so I was thankful I had found another close friend. He had actually become my new confidant.

Until this point, our relationship had been quite casual. But somewhere along the way, we had stopped using our nicknames. Our relationship had become more serious. I had stopped calling him "Little Patrick Henry" and he had stopped calling me "Cracker Jacks." I began to call him Calvin and he started to call me "Rete." Whenever we walked home together, he always carried my books. Once we were home, we usually stood outside and talked before I would go inside. But one afternoon, as we stood outside, my mother invited him to come in. She allowed us to sit in the living room and chat. After he left, my mother had a talk with me. Since I was almost sixteen, she told me that I was old enough to "take company." Most teenagers today don't go out on dates, as we did. Since my first edition, some 10 years, later teens enjoy each other on social media. They have *FaceTime*, Facebook, *Instagram, Snapchat, texting* and *messaging*. There are *some* teens who still love to hang-out with their friends at the movie and the malls. But most of them enjoy social media and probably have never heard this term used by my mother. In times past, when teenage girls were of age, they could invite that "special" young man to visit inside their homes, it was referred to as "taking company."

A few months later after that incident, my mother even told me I could go to a movie or a dance with him. My brother and some of our friends went with us. Until then, we usually stayed at home and listened to music. My mother had bought me and my sister a new stereo. She also bought some of the latest thirty-three albums and single forty-five RPM records. I couldn't imagine how she could afford it. I think she put them on *layaway* at the record shop downtown. She paid a small amount as a down payment. She then had to pay a certain percent each week until she paid the entire balance. The store owner kept the stereo until my mother paid off the balance; then she could bring the stereo home. My mother warned me, however, that if my grades dropped, I would lose my privilege of taking company, and she would confiscate our stereo as well. She also reminded me that there should be no "Hanky Panky" going on. She never told me what that meant, but somehow, I knew.

During these times, my mother seemed to be coping well. The psychiatrists said that for the moment, she was somewhat stable. Before then, she had not really been interested in my life. She simply did not have the strength to involve herself in what I did. But during my mid-teens, she became a little more involved in my life.

I wish my mother's mental state would have remained stable, but it never did. Within a two-year period, she had three more serious episodes. Each time she left the institution, she returned home with more medicine. She had medicine for depression, bipolar disorder, paranoia and schizophrenia, but sadly, she never had professional counseling. Eventually, she began to visit off site behavioral clinics. This way, they prescribed her medications, and she no longer had to be institutionalized which was a blessing, but I wish she could have gotten professional counseling to possibly help her resolve some of her issues rather than suppressing them. I really don't believe she was ever diagnosed correctly. These were very stressful times for all of my family. I was beyond thankful when she allowed me to have my boyfriend visit from time to time. I really needed the company of a "special" friend. Maybe my mother also felt I needed a friend at this point in my life. Mothers seem to know these things.

Calvin and I had many laughs, shared special moments, and enjoyed each other's company almost every day. Though we made some mistakes along the way, I am glad my mother allowed us to talk, share, and learn about each other. It helped us to build a healthy and lasting relationship. Many parents did not do that. But young boys and girls need to spend time with the opposite sex. This allows them to understand and prepare themselves to carry out God's plan of love and marriage between a male and female. This gives them hope in having children and building strong wholesome families. I learned a lot from my mistakes. But this is the not the only way God would have us learn. We should first trust in Him and not lean to our own understanding, and he will direct us. **Proverbs 3:5-6** If we did that, I am sure it would prevent us from making so many costly mistakes.

Something else wonderful happened during this time. I had another birthday. I turned sixteen! Calvin and I went fishing on my birthday. It was so much fun. This was my first fishing trip. I held my own. I caught two small fish and one baby turtle. Even though I couldn't swim, my boyfriend talked me into getting into a canoe. A water moccasin kept sticking his head out of the water, so for me it was time to go. I couldn't wait to get home. Suddenly, out of nowhere, I had the urge to see my friend Margie. Though we had not seen each other for some time, I still felt the need to share my special moments with her. This was one of those moments. We had both been so busy with other things lately, but I hoped to see her soon.

Gone Too Soon

One evening after I got home from school; I noticed my mother was acting rather strangely. She appeared to be sad and in deep thought. Not like the times before. This time something felt different. After my snack, I entered her room, and she asked me to sit on the bed next to her. She said she had something she needed to tell me. It sounded serious. She told me there had been a terrible accident, and Margie had been killed. She and a guy had been playing with a loaded gun and it accidentally went off, and she was killed instantly. She was dead. I couldn't believe it. I sat on the bed trying to recover my thoughts. I never told her about my wonderful fishing trip or any of the other events that had happened in my life. Several months had passed, and I had really wanted to visit her, but somehow, it seemed every time I decided to visit her, something always prevented me. Sometimes in life it's like that. Unfortunately, we find ourselves putting things off until it's too late. That is exactly what happened to me. I had planned to visit her, but it always seemed as though something would get in the way.

Margie had been killed, and I would never see her again. I had experienced some difficult times growing up, but this, by far, was one of the worst. This was my first experience with the death of someone so close to me. My mother just held me and told me we would visit the family later. I didn't know if I could go to the house knowing she was not there. At that time, I had so many mixed emotions. I was saddened because I did not take the opportunity to tell her I missed her and that we needed to visit more. I was also hurt by how she died. I wondered about the person who killed her, and it made me angry. Why would they be playing with a loaded gun? She was mature but still so young. I had so many questions and didn't know what to think. I hoped to get a better understanding of what happened when I visited her family.

Later that evening, my mother walked down to my girlfriend's house with me. Her family had moved on back street, again. I could barely go inside the house knowing that Margie was no longer there. I spoke with her mother for a few minutes and then went into the back room with the smaller children where I stayed for most of the evening comforting them. I braided the two smaller girls' hair. This made me feel that I was doing something special in honor of my friend. She always took pride in braiding her little sisters' hair.

My mother went into the bedroom with Margie's mother. They had both worked together as domestics in some of the same neighborhoods and had often helped each other to find work. They had been friends for many years. I knew my mother was saddened as well. While visiting and comforting the family, my mother began helping with a few household chores. After she finished cleaning the kitchen, she came and visited with the children for a bit. Then it was time for us to leave. I wanted to stay longer, but I knew it was getting late and we all needed some rest.

When I got home, I immediately dressed for bed. I lay in bed just staring at the ceiling and couldn't get to sleep. I just lay there thinking. I was so angry with myself for not visiting and hurt because I kept putting it off. Why did I keep putting it off? I tried to cry, but I couldn't even do that. The tears seemed to be stuck somewhere behind my eyelids, but they just wouldn't fall. I picked up a book, but I couldn't stay focused long enough to read. I closed my eyes hoping to get some sleep, but each time I closed them, I saw my girlfriend's face. My mind began to drift back to all of the evenings I had spent on the front porch with her. I remembered the games of Hopscotch, Jackstones, and Spin the Bottle. I began to smile when I thought about her teaching me to braid hair. I saw her hair flying in the wind as she jumped off of the banister of their front porch. I began to laugh as I saw her fall off the seesaw with her legs high up in the air. I laughed for a minute and then the tears came. Finally, I cried myself to sleep.

I had heard a scripture once that said: "*Weeping may endure for a night, but joy comes in the morning.*" **Psalm 30:5** It did not happen that way with me. That morning, when I opened my eyes, I felt sad and I could not remember why. I knew something was wrong, but I didn't know what. Then, it hit me. Margie was dead. I wanted it to be a bad dream, but it wasn't. I began to replay the conversation I had with my mother the evening before. The sick feeling, I experienced the day before was still lodged in my stomach while the sounds of her sisters' crying echoed in my head. This was no dream. It was real, and I questioned if I would ever get over this.

I don't know how I made it through the next few days. Even now, I struggle with the memory of her funeral. I know that I went to the funeral and walked down the aisle of the church, alongside her family. When I stopped at the coffin, there was a beautiful picture of my girlfriend placed on top. That is all I remember. I don't remember any of the service or even if I went to the gravesite. I'm sure I probably did, but sometimes people tend to blot out unpleasant memories. I only knew that a very significant chapter in my life had been closed, and all I had left were beautiful memories of the past. I would never forget my friend or the valuable lessons I learned from her during her lifetime. Even in death, she was still teaching me. She taught me not to put off things I should do today and that we do not know the plans God already has for our lives. I was always puzzled about the many things my girlfriend seemed to know at such a young age. It could have been that God allowed her to know and experience so many adult things early in life (such as taking care of a family) because He knew she would never raise a family of her own. Was she really gone too soon or was it just her time? Although there were a lot of things I failed to understand about Margie's death, this experience taught me many valuable lessons. Above all, I learned that whether we are young or old, we should never take life for granted. I came to understand the importance of living each day to its fullest for only God knows if it will be our last.

My Friend and I

(To Margie)

I had a very special friend
Who played around my tree.
We shared so many happy times
She meant the world to me.
I remember she seemed so grownup
To be a little girl
It seemed as if she'd lived her life
And conquered all the world.

She hurried home each day from school
To play the role of mother
With confidence, she'd go inside
To care for her sisters and brothers.
Sometimes, I'd ask her out to play
She'd shrug, then shake her head
"You'll have to wait; I can't go out
First I must make the beds."

She could handle so many grownup things
I hadn't yet learned to do
I was always somewhat mystified
At all the things she knew
How could she be a little girl
But yet seem so mature
I thought that she was "magical" back then I wasn't sure.

But now that I'm much older
I think I understand.
I'm sure that God had touched her
With His great powerful hand
I'm sure He let her travel roads
Unknown to other kids
I'm sure He opened doors to her
But to me He did forbid.

God wanted her to see the world
And enjoy it before she left
He wanted her to have a "taste of life"
Before she conquered death.

Retha Evans Ezell

Life Is Challenging:
The World is Changing

Months had passed, but I still missed Margie. Even though as she got older, we were not as close, I knew that I could go to her when I needed to talk to someone. Years after, I still felt the loneliness and pain. I tried to keep busy with activities hoping they would help me forget about her, but I don't think we ever forget those special people we lose through death. There is always a void left somewhere deep inside of us. I was thankful for my boyfriend having a listening ear. I know it was not easy for him either because their families had been neighbors for years. He knew them before I did. Many times, I would find myself reminiscing about the good times we all shared and would be overcome with grief. Somehow over the years, the bitter pain turned into sweet memories. Yet, life goes on. It seemed as though the more I thought backward, the faster my life moved forward. The world was rapidly changing and so was I.

I had already turned "Sweet Sixteen", but I didn't feel so sweet. It was in the middle of the sixties. Another year had passed, and I was convinced that the older I got, the more confused I became. I was uncertain about a lot of things. That year, I had faced several hardships and had to make some very difficult decisions. Being a teenager was challenging, and unfortunately, I had to try to understand the changes taking place in my life without the help of my mother. By then, my mother was institutionalized again. Her last mental bout was more severe than the others so the local clinic sent her back to the mental institution. At least we didn't have to go to live with anyone since my older sister was still living with us. She had not quite finished her college courses. Most weekends, she and her small children traveled back to the city, and I spent most of my weekends without any adult supervision.

During this time, I needed guidance, discipline, and supervision more than ever. I had begun to experience a lot of firsts. I had my first dance, my first experience with sex, my first real cigarette, and my first drink. I did not care for the taste of alcohol, and I did not want to drink because I saw the effect it had on my father. Some of my friends also tried marijuana, but I never tried that or any other drug. I smoked cigarettes because of my first job at my uncle's grocery store. At the grocery store, I had access to all kinds of cigarettes. I tried all of the many brands. Out of all the cigarettes on the shelf, I chose the one with the camel on the pack. I remembered that package from elementary school. It was the same brand that my father smoked. When I tried to take my first puff, I almost choked. I coughed every time I puffed.

When my father lived with us, he bought a carton of cigarettes every two weeks. I remember Al would sneak a pack and rearrange the package hoping my father wouldn't miss it. He would take a cigarette, light it, take a puff, and hold his breath; then he would call out all of our names. By the time he called all of our names and opened his mouth, little smoke rings would be floating in the air. This was enough entertainment to keep us from telling our parents. So, at an early age, my father and brother introduced me to cigarettes. It is interesting how family habits (good and bad) can be passed on to children. Though the cigarette I chose was the strongest of all, I chose it because it was my father's preferred smoke. There were at least seven other brands of cigarettes on the shelf (Pall Mall, Winston, Salem, Marlboro, L&M, Kent and Viceroy) in my uncle's store. I did not like the smell or taste of tobacco, so after a few months, I quit. I sold cigarettes to others, but I never had the urge to smoke again.

Now there are not just laws against minors selling and purchasing cigarettes, but new laws have been passed concerning "no smoking" in public places. If these laws had been passed during my teen years, I could not have worked in my uncle's store. It has been reported that cigarette smoking has dropped a lot since 2019. Vaping and e-cigarettes have taken the place of cigarette smoking among many adults and teens. Well, I am just thankful that during my teen years, I was able to have a job, because I really needed a job to help bring in extra income. I bought all of my school clothes and sometimes paid for my school and personal expenses. I even helped out with groceries for our family. We always needed sugar, milk, and bread.

Of all of my first experiences, I enjoyed my first job with my uncle the most. My uncle, Lonnie Louis Napier, chose me for the permanent job. My brother Hud was always giving everyone nicknames, so he named our uncle "Crow Bait." So, we all called him "Crow."

I enjoyed visiting with Uncle Lonnie, and we spent a lot of time together. I guess that could have been the reason he chose me for the job. He was always asking me questions about my schoolwork and other activities. He was always interested in education. He had been born blind, but it never hindered him from accomplishing his goals. He attended the blind academy nearby and went to the local college. My uncle graduated with honors with a major in Social Science and a minor in Business. In spite of his disability, he achieved great success.

He lived with my grandmother and ran a very profitable small business for years. He had opened his grocery store next to their home. My grandmother lived next door to my aunt and uncle. I never knew my maternal grandfather Freeman Napier because he died before I was born. But I was thankful to know my grandmother, particularly, because of my mother's illness, it was a blessing to have extended family living nearby. My grandmother was wonderful. She was full of wisdom and knowledge. She had only completed third grade, but she could read and write. Whenever she rested in bed, she always read her Bible and Dictionary. I enjoyed listening to her read and tell stories about all of my past relatives. She shared many interesting stories about our family. She told stories of how my great-grandparents came over as slaves. It seems that some of my grandparents' relatives were Blackfoot Indians. I also learned about the men in my family who had gone to war. Uncle Lonnie enjoyed her company too, but most of all, he enjoyed meeting other people. He loved to converse with them while they shopped for groceries and snacks. Everyone in the neighborhood knew him well. He even let them record "spots" for his radio commercials. He had a tape recorder under the candy counter, and he would record all of the children and adults who came to the store. The children especially enjoyed hearing themselves on tape. My job at my uncle's grocery store had a major impact on my life and was my most valuable real life adult experience.

There was another store nearby where I had my first dance. It was a long metal building so we named it the "Tin Can." It was a small store and a teen club combined. An older gentleman and his wife operated the store. He did not have as many items as my uncle, because he catered mostly to teens. He wanted to give the young people a place to hang out. He had a snack bar and an old jukebox with all of the latest hits we heard on the radio. I had my first dance swirling around the large wooden dance floor to those songs. Calvin taught me to slow drag and do the "Jitterbug" (Swing) at this little teen club. He would go to New York every summer and bring back the latest dances and teach them to us. We also created the "Griffin Line, Line Dance" in the late 60's, which was renamed the "Bus Stop" in the late '70's. The owner had a special affinity toward my boyfriend and me. He looked forward to our coming especially on weekends. He always waited until we arrived, and then he would slip a quarter in the jukebox. You could play three records for one quarter. We chose all of the latest hits from the Sixties such as Simon and Garfunkel's Sound of Silence, Ray Charles's Born to Lose, The Temptations' Ain't Too Proud to Beg, and The Beatles' I Want to Hold Your Hand. My boyfriend and I became dancing partners. We became so good at it that we even won several dance contests. We were a team. We had many hours of fun frequenting teen spots. There were several others around town. The owners were usually older couples who took good care of us. It was really nice clean fun. Those were the days! I always feel sad when I realize children of today do not have the same type of safe environment and fun games that we had. There are not many jackstones, ring games, hopscotch, sandlot football or local teen centers. Children today spend most of their time inside watching television, texting on their cell phones, playing video games or with some other computer gadget. Technology is necessary, but it has raised some concern, as it relates to our children. There are higher instances of childhood obesity and even more concern for our young people's safety, and ability to communicate without the use of technology. There is much to be said about "human contact." Children miss out on many enjoyable moments and interaction with other children. This could be the reason that some lack social skills and find it difficult to carry out healthy and long-lasting relationships.

Not all of my first experiences were positive. My experience with premarital sex had the most detrimental effect on my life. Over the years, I was taught many things at home, school, and church, but I was never really educated about marriage and sex. During my teen years, there were no classes on these subjects. Today, many community organizations and even some churches provided workshops on these issues and more. I have personally taught sexual education classes for various community organizations. However, parents had to sign a consent form for their children because many parents nowadays would rather teach their own children about these sensitive matters.

These are opportunities and advantages afforded to the new generations that my generation did not have. But even if I had the training and information, I cannot say for certain I would have taken advantage of it or changed my behavior. However, I do believe what we are taught (or even not taught) plays a vital role in shaping our everyday lives. The things we are taught can at least give us the information we need to make positive decisions, if we choose to do so. I would like to have been given more information on relationships, marriage, and sexual matters, so I could have made more informed decisions. This is not an excuse for my actions, but just insight gleaned from counseling youth for many years. Knowledge *is* power if you take advantage of it, once received.

Though I attended church almost every Sunday, I can remember only one sermon preached about sex. I remember hearing a sermon preached about the woman who committed adultery. The only thing emphasized in the message was the fact that the woman was forgiven. I had never heard nor was I even familiar with the word "fornication" until I was in my early twenties. I know that may sound ridiculous, but it's true.

Even in attending school, I cannot recall having any classes on sex education. I did have a health teacher who showed us a film on STD's (Sexually Transmitted Diseases). The film was brief and afterwards, the female teacher had a session with the girls about personal hygiene while the male teacher had a separate session for the boys. I am not sure of the information they received in their session. There are many opinions and debate of whether schools should be allowed to provide sex education classes. Some say sex education is the parents' responsibility; however, when I was a teen, the subject of sex was "taboo" for many parents.

The only sex education lesson I received from my mother were the words: "There better be no hanky panky" and "You had better not mess up and break your leg". When a mother told her daughter not to "mess up" or "break her leg", it meant not to get pregnant before she was married. My mother told me if I messed up, she was going to kill me. These were all exaggerations, but she was really serious about the matter. There were many life factors that led to my engaging in sex before marriage, but in the end, the choice was mine. These wrong choices greatly impacted my life. Since I did not have any useful, information, and guidance I needed during my teen years, I now spend most of my time educating, advising, and counseling youth on critical life choices. I created a daily abstinence meditation kit and CD entitled, "Spread the Word! "Love Like Dove!" I have also presented workshops locally and internationally in Africa. I conducted workshops in Nakuru and Nairobi, Kenya at schools and AIDS infected neighborhoods. Over the past ten years, I visited and taught in several other countries, cities and states. Like me, and even now many children do not have parents around or "good" information to inform them or educate on sexual matters. In Africa, they really needed and appreciated the resources and information they received to make the right choices during their critical years. *Edu-Serc* in Maryland, CEO *Brian Smith* presented me with their *(Educator Serving the Community Award)* for these teachings. I did teach a few groups on abstinence, but over the last 10 years abstinence is almost unheard of in today's society. There may be some churches and maybe some parents who still encourage abstinence, but some teach safe-sex, instead. I guess this is due to societal changes.

But I can say without actually using the word my mother wanted us to abstain. But as I grew older, she had less time to discipline, as she continued to slip back into a very deep depression. She stayed in bed all day trapped in her own little world of living in the past. She could not move forward. She tried, but it seemed that she would always return into a world of loneliness and despair. As I matured spiritually, I realized that my mother needed to forgive herself and others. She needed the courage and strength of mind to forgive. But how do we come upon this courage and strength? A forgiving spirit does not come easily. Our minds must first be transformed before one's spirit can be renewed. Once we think we have a right to be angry, unforgiving, and bitter, it is difficult to let go of the past. It is difficult to look toward the future. *Philippians 3:14* declares that we must forget about those things which are behind us and reach toward those things which are before us. My mother had become drenched in past hurts and disappointments that clouded her hope for the future. Though there were opportunities in place for her to complete her education, she would not or could not move forward. She was still blaming her father for not allowing her to finish school. Though she was a very kind and attractive woman, she could never have a healthy relationship because she was still angry with my father. She was stuck in the past. She had so many inner hurts that she was constantly filled with grief. She was actually afraid to experience happiness. She was not strong enough to help herself, so she certainly was not strong enough to help me at that particular time in my life. Yet, no matter what my mother went through, I never doubted her love for me at that particular time in my life. In the end, the choice was mine and mine alone.

We all know that our choices have consequences. Having hours of free time, and being unsupervised, by the time I was seventeen, I saw Calvin more than anyone else. We were together at home and school. My fate was almost inevitable. As time moved swiftly, my school days had become very hectic and were nearing an end.

By now, I was already a junior in high school. At the end of my junior year, I received a letter in the mail asking if I would like to attend a segregated high school as a "Freedom of Choice" student. "Freedom of Choice" was a plan that many states developed during the mid1960's aimed at integrating schools. Without thinking, I accepted. I guess I wanted a change. About sixty other African American students from my school also accepted the program. My sister was one of them. She was an upcoming junior and I would be entering my senior year. I would have to experience one year of early integration. One of my former classmates also attended as a senior. I guess one could say that we were the pioneers of school integration in the South.

After enjoying yet another summer that passed far too quickly, it was now time to step onto the bus to my new school. All of the white students on the bus had allegedly formed a pact that they would not let a black person sit on the seat with them. Though there were many empty seats, I chose to stand up until I got to school. Once I was inside of the building, reality set in. I had no friends at this school. This was my senior year, and I would graduate with a group of people whom I did not know. What in the world was I thinking?

When I entered my first class, all of the student's conversation ended abruptly. There were several empty seats. However, after my early morning bus experience, I was reluctant to sit. There was one young man who smiled, so I chose the seat next to him. I waited for his reaction. Surprisingly, he just winked at me.

Finally, the teacher entered the classroom. She asked everyone to open their books. I was a new student and had not purchased all of my books. The young man next to me handed me his book. He slid over closer to the girl on the other side of him and looked on with her. At least a smile and a book were a good start. His small act of kindness opened the door for many of the other students to share their books and sometimes school supplies with me. I will always remember him. His name was *Tommy.*

That particular year taught me that people really do share lot more similarities than they are willing to admit. Also, one small act of kindness can become a bridge that connects all races, genders, and nationalities. Most of all, I learned that a smile is heartwarming and comforting no matter the color of the face. By the end of the year, we were all just students trying to complete our coursework for graduation. Of course, there was no real socialization between us, but I didn't have a problem with that. We had very little time to socialize anyway. As it was, the year was quickly coming to a close, and I would be graduating soon. It seemed like my life sprinted in full speed, and before I knew it, I was almost eighteen.

My life was in a whirlwind, and so was the rest of the world. It was the sixties, and it wasn't just chaos in my own "little world", but in our country, as well. In 1963, John Fitzgerald Kennedy, the 39th President of the United States, was assassinated. He was the youngest of all presidents ever elected in this country. This is also the period that Dr. Martin Luther King, Jr. led the "Civil Rights Movement." There were incidents of water hosing, boycotting, rioting, bombings, and shootings, and this was a time of violence and racial unrest. The sixties were also the "Vietnam Era." Thousands of young men were being shipped overseas to Vietnam to fight in a war. Many were killed and sent back home to be buried. Many families were saddened. Since I published my first edition, surely, we are living in even more turbulent times of wars (Ukraine, Israel), lawlessness in a world of great "racial divide and in national policy, along with virus outbreaks (Covid-19) throughout the world. It truly is a critical time to be entering into adulthood, and to be an adult. *There are wars and rumors of wars, nation against nation, kingdom against kingdom, famines, pestilences, and earthquakes in various places.* **Matthew 24** But we know that God is faithful. **Lamentations 3:22-23**

Illustrated by: Lola Ragin Morrow

Grandmothers

(To Big Mama, Lucy Wynn Napier)

Grandmothers are always nice to have
They're filled with wisdom and poise
They tell sweet stories of years gone by
That everyone enjoys.

They help you trace your heritage
And outline your family tree
In their family Bible
A list of names you see.

They remember every name inside
They tell you who they are
They show you ribbons and medals
From relatives who went to war.

Grandmother's offer lots of advice
But we never take offense
I guess it's because we respect their wit
And good ole' common sense.
Because grandmothers are precious gems carved with God's own hands

Grandmothers will never become extinct
They're always be in demand.

Retha Evans Ezell

Section Three

Love Leaps Forward

And now abide faith, hope, love, these three;
but the greatest of these is love.

(I Corinthians 13:13)

Growing Up is Hard to Do!

*When I was a child, I spoke as a child, I understood
as a child, I thought as a child; but when I became
a man, I put away childish things.*

(I Corinthians 13:11)

Welcome to Adulthood

I finally celebrated my eighteenth birthday. I was a "proud senior" waiting to graduate. I had no idea my senior year would be so expensive. I was so thankful that I had a job; otherwise, I could not have afforded to buy the many items I needed. Yearbooks had already been compiled the year before, so I did not pay for one of those. Of course, they included my senior picture, and I was a part of the group picture. It was the worst picture I had ever taken. I was never photogenic, but that one was awful. I was relieved that my individual picture turned out okay. We all had to place our philosophy of life next to our photo, but I have since forgotten what I wrote. It was something about cream "rising" to the top.

Graduation was not what I expected. Because of various incidents that happened during the school year, I was not overly excited like the other students. There was a certain camaraderie on graduation night among all of the graduates. For the first time, some of the students who had never spoken to me wanted to talk. Though we attended class together, we never interacted outside of class. One girl who had constantly snubbed me the entire year helped to straighten my tassel. When they gave out honors and my name was called, the entire class cheered. As everyone continued to cheer, I finally got into the spirit of the ceremony. My mother, sisters, and brothers were there. They were all ecstatic. After graduation, my classmates gathered around for refreshments and discussed our future plans. Many of them had received scholarships. I was an honor graduate, but I did not know if I would be able to attend college. Since I had changed schools, I did not have an advocate seeking funds for my education.

I did not receive any college information during my senior year. Many of the students said they would be going to the college where their parents attended. I could not relate to that. Neither of my parents even graduated from high school. In my past occupation, I assisted middle and high school "first" generation students with *TRIO programs (Educational Talent Search)*. I encouraged them and gave them information, and I also assisted them in seeking funding so that they may attend a postsecondary institution. I probably was led to this field of work because of my own experience. Even as a retiree, I still encourage and assist young people in pursuing their educational goals. Many of the students are the first to attend a postsecondary institution in their families.

After my high school graduation, I can recall talking to my friends from my old high school. Most of them, including my boyfriend, were prepared to begin college in early fall. And there I was, at a crossroads with no sense of what direction to take. I had spent twelve years of studying and working hard to get the best grades and did not know what next. I had no clue of what to do during the next stage of my life.

Since I was not attending college, I had to seek employment. I accepted a job babysitting and worked for a year. The next year, my sister graduated from high school and was in the same situation as mine. When a counselor from our old high school found out we were not in college, she sought funding for us. She went to a local women's group and asked for funds for our tuition. They also gave us money for books. We attended the local college, and I was so excited. I was really grateful for the organization's help and I wrote them several "Thank You" notes throughout the year. I always inserted a copy of my grades. My boyfriend was also enrolled at the same college. It was fun being in school with him again. We would put fifty cents worth of gas in his mother's 1957 blue and white Bonneville and ride to school for days. Gas was only fifty cents per gallon. Times have really changed. Since that time, gas prices have skyrocketed sometimes more than $6.00 per gallon.

At the end of my freshmen year, my boyfriend asked me to marry him. He gave me a very simple engagement ring, but I was overjoyed. He said once he got a job, he would get me a more expensive one, but that was not important to me. He was no longer my boyfriend but now my fiancé. Again, my excitement did not last very long. Again, another *swift transition.* The very next week, he received a draft notice in the mail. However, he was given a choice to make a decision to enlist in a special two-year program with the Navy or be drafted into the army. He decided to enlist. Once again, my life leaped into full speed. A few weeks after his enlistment, I began to feel very ill. I thought it was nervous tension. My stomach was upset, and I started to sleep a lot. My next-door neighbor and friend "Popcorn" asked me if I was expecting. She had a sister who had recently given birth, so she was familiar with the symptoms. She finally convinced me to go to for an examination. She was right, I was four months pregnant. I definitely had to get married now. In the sixties, it wasn't popular or acceptable to be pregnant outside of marriage. It was not as it is today. It seems like society sometimes popularizes and even promotes different types of families. I wanted to tell my mother, but she was still dealing with her depression. What was I thinking? A baby, no money, and no husband. I didn't even know how to break the news to my fiancé.

I knew he was already under a lot of stress. He was still grieving the loss of his father who had died a month before we graduated. Early one Sunday morning in April 1967, both Calvin and his father joyfully said their "goodbyes" (not knowing it would be their last). Calvin went to the "Elks Lodge" to give his noted oration ("Give Me Liberty or Give Me Death"), by Patrick Henry, while His father went off to church to preach his regular 11:00 A.M. sermon. However, immediately after the message his father had a massive heart attack and died. Of course, this had been very devastating to his family and him. This was also devastating to him because he knew that his father was looking forward to his only son graduating from high school. My husband and his father had a very close relationship. His father was the sole provider at that time, but he had joined him running the family painting business.

In spite of all of his family problems, I knew I had to tell him about the pregnancy. I had no idea of how he would react. I told him a few weeks before he left for basic training. The night I told him he had very little to say. As we sat together on our favorite chair, he was quiet and stared at the wall. Finally, he asked me what I would like to do. When he asked me if I still wanted to get married, my heart sank. From hearing those questions, I realized he had already changed his mind about marriage. He waited for my response. I didn't respond because I knew he already knew the answer. It was obvious that something had changed since the last time we talked. We were engaged before I knew I was expecting. So, I just sat and waited for him to explain. We sat silently for hours, which was a first for us. We had always had so much to say to one another.

Finally, the silence was broken. He came and sat closer to me and told me he really wanted to marry me, but he had other household obligations at home. I sat silently holding back the tears. I wanted to be compassionate and sympathetic because I truly understood, but what about me and the baby I was carrying? Who would take care of us? He assured me that he loved me, and it would work out. He ended the conversation and said we would talk later.

The next week we had a long talk. He had to report to Jacksonville, Florida the following week. He told me he loved me and would write to me every day and as soon as he was settled, he would send money for my care. He asked me to please wait for him, and we would make plans to get married the following year. Though this was not what I wanted to hear, I accepted his proposal.

From this experience, I learned the consequences of having sex before marriage. As a result of my choices, I was left alone with no job, no income, and not even a boyfriend to keep me company or help me during these trying times. Nevertheless, I still loved him. I had heard somewhere that love covers a multitude of sins. I later learned that this statement was scriptural. The scripture in *I Peter 4:8* states that we must have a fervent love for one another, for love covers a multitude of sins. Even though my husband and I made some bad decisions, I knew we both loved and cared for one another. We had shared a lifetime of experiences together, both good and bad. We had built a very strong and lasting relationship with one another, and I knew in my heart that he was the man that God had chosen as my husband, and I could not see myself married to anyone else.

The question was whether I should wait for him or insist that we get married. I knew there was the possibility he might meet someone else while he was away. I had seen many girls broken hearted after they waited for their boyfriend or fiancé to return home from service only to learn that they had found someone else. Many thoughts went through my mind. I had personal concerns of my own, but I was also concerned about him. The country was in the midst of war, and I wondered if he would be shipped to Vietnam. Like his mother, I too was fearful that he may not return home. I had two former classmates who had already been killed in Vietnam. So that was always on my mind.

But my most *pressing* concern was how I would raise a child alone. I was overwhelmed and afraid. I had no idea of what pregnancy or raising a child looked like. I didn't know how I was going to pay for a physician and hospital bills without insurance or government assistance. I could only hope that my fiancé would soon be in a position to help. Nevertheless, I had to make some major decisions, and I needed to do so quickly. Time was of the essence. In a few months, I would have a baby who would need my love, affection, and financial support. Therefore, I knew I had to make preparations for the challenging times ahead.

One Nation Under God

(To America)

The "Reds," the 'Yellows,' the "Blacks," the "Whites"
Must learn to love each other.
We can't bring peace to the rest of the world
Unless we live as brothers.
We must begin to look beneath
The colors of our skin.
We must begin to search for qualities
Embedded deep within.
We don't have time to waste our thoughts
On prejudice and hate.
Our nation needs this energy
To achieve, invent, create.

We must begin to respect each other
It shouldn't be that hard.
If we are striving to become
"One Nation Under God!"
The Declaration, The Constitution, also the Bill of Rights
The Statue of Liberty, Ellis Island and our forefathers who had to
fight.
These are constant reminders
That played a major part.
In helping our country to become
"One Nation Under God!"

Retha Evans Ezell

Off to the City

After carefully weighing the few options I had, I made a decision to leave home and move to the city with my older brother. I had always wanted to live in Atlanta. Ever since my mother and little sister had stayed in the city, I had a desire to go there. Though the circumstances were unpleasant, my chance had finally come. My brother had gotten married, so I went to live with him, his wife, and two small children. I became their live-in babysitter. Moving away also helped because I would not have to answer too many unsolicited questions. Many parents actually sent their daughters away to live with relatives when they became pregnant out of wedlock. I guess it was somewhat like Joseph and Mary in the Bible. Joseph didn't want to make a public example of Mary, so he made plans to put her away secretly. Many parents would put their daughters away secretly, but I chose to go on my own. Back then, there was a certain stigma attached to girls having children out of wedlock. I don't think they even call it that anymore. Now, it is simply called teen pregnancy. Though I regretted getting pregnant, I was thankful I had finished high school and didn't disappoint my mother in that respect. She wanted all of her children to graduate from high school. This did not make the mistake any more acceptable, but at least it would be helpful now that I was seeking employment.

In today's society, it is significantly more acceptable to have children out of wedlock. Pregnant teens can attend school, and in some places, there are schools for pregnant mothers. That was unheard of in my day. They even have a television show dedicated to teen pregnancy. Teen pregnancy has almost become a fad. There are some girls who say they get pregnant so they can receive governmental assistance to help them move into their own place. Others say they just want someone to love. They dress up their little infants and treat them like dolls. I encounter many young girls who take great pride while passing their sonograms around to their friends. They wear short tops and proudly flaunt their bellies. In spite of the fact that there are many birth control methods available, many teenagers choose not to take advantage of them. Presently in some areas, birth control methods are offered to children without parental consent. In my generation, this was not possible. Yet, I truly believe that the only sure and safe birth control is abstinence. I wish I had known then what I know now, but at least I am able to use my own experiences to share with other young girls.

I only stayed with my brother for about four months. As I came closer to giving birth, I decided to return home. I spent most of my days with my God family "Mother Lillie", Veronica/*William*, John/*Dot*). I also had 3 other god sisters, *Doris, Brenda* and *Sonja*. A few weeks after I returned home, I went in labor and didn't even know it. When I told "Popcorn" what was happening, she called for my godbrother, John and he took me to the hospital. He rushed me to the hospital and remained with me. My younger sister *(Peanut)* was apprehensive, so she stayed at home. In the delivery room, I had prepared myself for the worst, but it never came. In fact, it all happened rather quickly.

Within a few hours, our son was born. He was a healthy 6 lbs.9 oz. Calvin could not be there because he was traveling overseas, somewhere in the Caribbean and Mediterranean. I could not contact him to tell him about our son. At that time, that really didn't concern me. I was just glad it was over. When it was time for my dismissal, my mother signed the paperwork and paid the hospital bill.

When I left the hospital, I had no idea what I would do with this little creature. Notice, I did not say "bundle of joy." He did not feel like a bundle of joy, but rather this was someone who needed care and I did not know I could provide it. As they wheeled me out to the lobby for pick up, I really did not know what to do with this bundle wrapped in swaddling clothes. I was really afraid and with good reason. Since the baby arrived three weeks early. I was totally unprepared. I had left my room in a mess and did not have anything for our son. My body was aching and the baby was crying. I thank God that the hospital had given me a package of items for him. I had a several cans of formula, bottles, and a few diapers. I had to read the directions in order to mix the formula because I had never taken care of a baby before. The nurses fed him while we were in the hospital. In times past, the nurses kept the infant in the nursery and the mother watched through the window as the nurses fed the baby. There was not much bonding between mother and infant before they arrived home. When my time of bonding came, I felt it came too soon. The first time, I was nervous when I fed him. I was afraid he would get choked. When he finished the bottle, I was relieved. Shortly afterwards, he started to cry. Instinctively, I knew to check his diaper, and it definitely needed to be changed. I pulled a diaper from the gift bag and changed him. When I finished, he looked at me and he appeared to have a cute little smile. I believe he stared at me as if to say, it was going to be okay. He looked up at me and I felt that with his little innocent eyes he was giving me instructions for his care: When I am hungry, feed me, and when I am wet, change me. It's simple. Moments later, he closed his eyes and drifted off to sleep. When I looked down at him, he still had the smile on his face. I put my finger in his hand and I could not believe that he clutched it. We were one. We were in this thing together.

Immediately, right before my eyes, this fragile little creature, wrapped in swaddling clothes emerged into a "bundle of joy." From that moment on, I was hooked. Again, just one little "smile" had made all the difference in the world. It gave me hope and encouragement to pick up the pieces, head back to the city, and bravely face a new set of challenges.

Time to Move Forward

After I got the baby settled, my mother came in and handed me a large stack of letters from Calvin. He had promised he would write me every day and he had. Since he was traveling overseas there was a delay in the mail. I had sent several letters to him, but had not heard from him in months. We had shared letters during his basic training so I knew there was a lapse in the mail, but not like this. He had written some of the letters more than a month before I received them. In each letter, he wanted to know if he had a son yet. He had predicted that the baby would be a boy. He had also told me that he wanted to name him *Antonio*. I had written Calvin as soon as our son, Antonio, was born, but obviously he had not received my letters. It took quite a while for me to finish reading all of my mail. When I opened my last letter, there was money inside and I used it to buy items for the baby. The letters and money were a pleasant surprise that came at a time when I really needed some emotional and financial support. Afterwards, I sat down and wrote a letter with a picture inside for the new "Papa." In my letter, I also told him that I had made a decision to move back to Atlanta with my brother in a few months.

When my son was four months old, I called my older brother and asked him if I could return to Atlanta to live with him. He told me that I could move back whenever I wanted. It took only a few weeks to pack and get things in order. It was truly a blessing to have family members who were willing to help during our time of need. I enjoyed staying in the city with my brother Wint and his family. After living with them for a few months, I became less anxious and gained a sense of security. They were happy to have us, and they enjoyed having a new baby in the home. They all helped me to take care of my son. Since they were already parents, I learned a lot from them. I really enjoyed staying home with my baby, but I knew it was time for me to look for work.

After my son was six months old, I decided to look for work. One of the reasons I left home was the lack of job opportunities where I lived. There were few jobs in my hometown for young African American females without a college degree, so quite a few went into homes to work as a domestic. I was told that there were much greater opportunities in the city. I was also thankful I had obtained a few hours of college credit before I became pregnant. Hopefully, this would work in my favor and help to land me a decent job. Both my brother and his wife worked outside of the home during the day, so we decided that I would search for a job at night so we could share in babysitting all the children in the home.

Since I didn't know where to begin my job search, I called my brother-in-law (Douglas/*Cat)* who had developed a network of friends and businessmen in the area. Just as I hoped, he was able to assist me. He called one of his associates at a famous local restaurant (*Paschal Bros.)* where he usually ate lunch with a group of friends. The restaurant had an opening they needed to fill immediately. My brother-in-law drove me to the restaurant the following day to complete my application. They needed a full-time counter clerk. Since I had worked as a cashier and salesperson at my uncle's store, I was confident I could handle the job.

I entered a small office with a big glass window. An older gentleman read over my application, looked at me, and handed me an orange uniform and brown apron with a wide pocket. "Does this mean I'm hired?" I asked. "Sure does," he said. He told me I would work the evening shift for eight hours and some weekends. I normally went in around three and left at eleven. This worked well with my brother and sister-in-law's schedule. I started work the next day. I was now gainfully employed.

My first day was a breeze. Along with another cashier, I waited on customers at the counter. Most of the evening customers only wanted coffee and donuts or apple pie. When they finished drinking a twenty-five-cent cup of coffee, they would leave me seventy-five cents which I thought was odd. I began to have the same customers come back every evening. Because there were several universities in the area, college professors and students would give me fifty cents just for taking their short orders quickly. When the professors ate lunch at my counter, I would usually receive one dollar. By the end of my shift, I would have at least twenty dollars in my apron pocket. In addition, I received a small base salary from my employer.

My brother could not wait for me to come home so he could count my money. He asked me how I made so much money just working at a counter. I couldn't answer him because I didn't know the answer. I just spoke to each customer, treated them with kindness and gave them their orders as quickly and correctly as I could. As the months passed, my nightly income had increased a few more dollars. I thought this was normal until the other owner called me to his office.

I had only spoken to the one of the brothers who hired me. The other gentleman sat quietly at his desk and began using his calculator. He looked up and made me an offer for more money if I would "work the floor" of the motor hotel. He told me when he had good waitresses, he tried to move them up to the restaurant dining and entertainment area where they could make more money. The restaurant was attached to the hotel, and I had heard rumors that girls working the floor were often propositioned by traveling businessmen and entertainers. In any case, I was told that the floor waitresses had to be extremely cautious because some of the girls had lost their jobs after fraternizing with the customers. Whether the rumors were true or not, I did not want to put myself in that position. Some would say this could have been a great opportunity for me, but be that as it may, I would have had to work longer hours, spend less time with my son, and it would not work with our babysitting schedule.

So, without any consideration of the money, I immediately rejected the offer. He was not very pleased. He insisted that I could make more money and have a more promising position. Yet, I still declined. Anyway, I had come to like my job at the counter, and I would miss talking with my regular customers. There was Mr. Banks who was a barber. Then, there was Mr. Barnes with his shoe shine kit and Lucille, a hairdresser. They needed to have a smile and cup of coffee handed to them with love at the end of the day. All of my customers knew I was supposed to be moved to the floor, before I did. They were excited when they found out I didn't take the job and to my pleasant surprise, my tips increased.

But the very next week things changed. My brother's shift changed and he could no longer keep my son. I would have to hire a babysitter. I could not handle my expenses and pay a babysitter off the meager salary I earned. Though my tips had increased, this was not enough to take care of my responsibilities, bus fare, and daycare. Daycare was very expensive in the city. If I couldn't find a babysitter, I would have to return home, and I certainly did not want to do that. I moved to make a better life for me and my son. I had just begun to move forward and had no intentions of moving backward. Decisions! Decisions! Decisions! I knew I had to make one soon. My brother's shift would start the following week and I needed a miracle.

I Believe in Miracles!

I was thankful I did not have to move back home. I found another job right in the nick of time. This job was with an insurance company. I found it in the local newspaper. In the '70s, all I had to do was call the company and they told me when to come in for an interview. I just went to the company and was hired the same day. Even over the past ten years, job searching has changed. Job searches are online, just as almost everything else is. You must have a cell phone or access to a computer. However, after Covid-19 pandemic there was a labor shortage and millions of workers did not reenter the job market and many businesses had to begin hiring onsite. Some businesses even had to close.

Well, I am just grateful that at least the job market was somewhat stable, during my young adult years. I quickly landed and accepted the job as a file clerk. The salary was low and by the time taxes were taken out, I made just enough to pay for a few things I needed. I did receive benefits, so I was thankful and confident we would be fine. Somehow these various work experiences helped me to become more self-confident.

My self-confidence and independence carried over into the workplace. Within a few months, I had moved up very quickly on my job. The office manager created a search clerk position for me since whenever someone could not find a missing file, I could. All day long I took a list of all of the lost insurance files and combed the offices until I found them. I stayed at this company for about nine months. It was a long commute from my home, so I had to leave at five in the morning to make it to work by eight; however, at that time, it was the best I could do. Sometimes in life we have to take the lesser in order to obtain the greater. For me, this was one of those times.

One evening after work, I met one of my coworkers from the restaurant. She told me about a job downtown that was much closer to my home. I applied for the position and within a few days, I was working downtown at a major insurance corporation as a mail clerk. I enjoyed the work, and I did not have to leave home as early. I could actually see my son off to the babysitter. Usually, I would leave home before he got up in the morning and my brother would be responsible for getting him ready for daycare.

My first morning of seeing him off turned out to be a nightmare. The babysitter blew the horn and I ran outside to take my son. There was a long tan station wagon waiting outside. When she opened the door, I was appalled. The car was overrun with infants and children. There were babies in carriers and car seats in the back windows and all over the seats and the floors. After scolding the babysitter, I took my son inside and never sent him there again. I asked my brother if he knew there were babies stacked in the sitter's station wagon. He said that she usually came to the door and he handed her my son, so he had not been aware. I did not know what I was going to do.

I would have to call my son's paternal grandmother who still lived in my hometown to keep him while I worked. If not, I would have to quit my new job and return home. Many times, parents have to put the safety and welfare of their children above everything else.

Therefore, after confronting the babysitter that morning, I called my supervisor and explained my situation. She was very understanding and allowed me to take one day of emergency leave. I explained the situation and solicited her help. His grandmother was excited to have him spend some time with her. She had seen him only a few times since he was born. When I took my son to live with her, I had a short visit with my mother and sister. Both families were excited that I was leaving the baby. I knew my sister was still in school, and I never really knew how long my mother would remain stable. However, my family said that they would be available if his grandmother needed them. This was very comforting for me. I said my goodbyes and took an early bus back to Atlanta so I could get prepared for the next day.

Once I returned, it did not take very long for me to realize I missed my son. Within a few months, I was ready to quit my job and head back home. It would be uncomfortable returning home because the perception was that when a person left home and had to return, no matter the reason, people usually thought she was a failure. However, I missed my son and had no time to concern myself with public opinion. His grandmother had done a wonderful job taking care of him but I missed him very much. I needed a miracle. I prayed that something would happen so I could be united with my baby. Reluctantly, I decided to turn in my resignation and return home.

God must have heard my prayer. By the time I had spent most of my money, I received a letter from my fiancé telling me that he would be discharged from the military within a few weeks. I couldn't believe it! He had just returned to the base after taking a three week leave for Christmas. We had been marking our calendars daily as we counted down the days that he still had left. When he signed up with the Navy, he was in a special two-year program. (USS Suribachi, AE-21) He had at least six more months left to serve but he said the military gave him an opportunity to re-enlist with a bonus or opt out of the military. He chose to opt out. I was ecstatic, but very much in disbelief. The moment I had been waiting for was finally here. I had faith that something would come through, though I did not know it would happen so soon. God really is an "on time" God. He is indeed a miracle worker. He shows Himself mighty over and over, again.

Within a few weeks, Calvin came home. I was staying with my mother. My older sister and younger brother had both graduated from the local college. There was no one at home now but me, my sister and my son. At this time, my mother was somewhat stable. When my fiancé arrived home, he came over to see our son, and he asked my mother if he could marry me. Of course, she told him yes. This time he gave me a beautiful wedding band with diamond shaped etchings, and asked me to marry him, I was nervous and a little skeptical. I thought something would go wrong. After all, he had asked me to marry him before, and it didn't happen. In spite of everything, my answer was yes. No matter the circumstances, we still loved and cared for each other as always. I truly believed that we had been ordained by God to be together, and we were mates for life.

Not long ago, I read an article about doves. The article described that doves mate for life and take care of their young together. Looking back, this is how I saw the two of us. Like two doves sitting on an olive branch, we had been summoned. God had pre-destined us to become mates for life. This time, we were to build the nest which we had started with honor, especially since I had found out that I was expecting again. This baby was to share the same birth month as our son who was born in September. In spite of our sins, God had blessed us and answered our prayers.

I have learned that God is merciful, but He is also a God of righteousness and judgment *Jeremiah 9:23-24* We cannot continue to sin and think that God will continue to keep us without consequences. Love does cover a multitude of sins, but that does not give us the right to continue in sin. I had already made up my mind that if my fiancé did not propose as soon as he returned home, I would regretfully have to end our relationship. At some point, we must take a good look at ourselves and admit that what we are doing is wrong in the sight of God, and sin is detrimental to our lives and the lives of others, so it is necessary to change our ways. *Romans 12:1-2* I realized that there were serious consequences for our sins, and sometimes we could stray away so far that it is difficult to find our way back to God. I saw this happening to my fiancé and me. Yet, God had a plan for our lives in spite of the mistakes we made.

God knew we were like two turtle doves prone to wander, but by His grace we found our way back to Him. I was thankful to know if we confessed our sins, He was faithful and just to forgive us and cleanse us from all unrighteousness *I John 1:9*. God had called us into marriage and to become parents. We had a God-given responsibility to carry out His ordinance of raising and providing for our children until they were independent. *Whenever that is!*

Building Our Nest

This time it really did happen. On a beautiful sunny day in May, we were married. We didn't have a wedding. We went before a very kind judge who counseled us and talked like a preacher. Maybe he was. I still remember his very stern words as he asked us, "Do you promise to stay together in good times and bad times, for better or for worse, in sickness and in health, for richer or for poorer, until death do you part?" We both individually answered that we would. With a quick hug and smack on the lips, we were off to the fish creek to celebrate our honeymoon.

Ironically, we started our marriage exactly as we did our first date (on the fish creek). We went back to our favorite fishing hole and enjoyed every minute. Only this time, "There were three of us!" Technically, there were four. We did not let this dampen our spirits. We really enjoyed our family outing together. With very few funds, it was nothing elaborate, but we had a wonderful time. This probably would have been some bride's first argument with her new husband, but not mine. It did not matter where we spent our honeymoon. I was just happy to be married to my first and only love. I was delighted to have my best friend and confidant home so that we could become a real family.

My excitement was short-lived. Before I knew it, we had been ushered out of our hour of marital bliss into the first signs of marital growing pains. Once we were married, we moved in with my mother. Most of my husband's military saving was almost depleted. He had not had a lot of success in finding a job. After a few months, my husband decided that it would be better for us to move in with his mother since she lived alone. Since he hadn't found work, I am sure he felt better living with his mom. Though I knew I would feel more comfortable living with my own mother, we agreed to move in with his mother. ***Ruth 1:16-17*** The months moved by swiftly and before I knew it, I was in labor. I went into labor on "Labor Day". I was certainly hoping for a girl, but I had another boy. Back then, I was not even aware of a sonogram to tell you the gender of the child beforehand, I am sure there was, but we surely could not afford it. Our new baby was healthy. He had fat cheeks and curly hair. We named him Jacques Calvett which was his father's name in French. I was not as nervous this time as I was with my first child. I was relieved that my husband was by my side during labor and would be there to help me with our baby when we returned home.

The following months were more challenging than we expected. Funds were very limited. During this time, it was no different than it is now for military veterans. It is a struggle returning to civilian life. My husband only served for a short time, but some veterans serve for years and defend us in war and still face insurmountable challenges once they return home. Though we have made some strides in assisting veterans, there is more work needed to assist returning veterans and their families. Many have come to understand that returning home after serving one's country causes major adjustments for the veterans and their families. It took us both quite some time to get adjusted to his return. Picking up where we left off was not easy.

Eventually, we received a breakthrough, but it was not exactly what my husband wanted. He obtained a job at a local plant, the very place he did not want to work. He had to work very long hours and the job was quite demanding. Nevertheless, he had to accept the job because he had a family now. He was no longer that callow fellow I mooned over some years ago. It was time to grow up. Like a dove, he would just have to begin providing for his young. And of course, as his mate, I would have to assist him as much as I could.

After a few months, we found a shabby little house, and we moved. His mother needed her space, but we knew we would miss her. We visited her almost everyday. My husband also obtained another job and happily left the plant. We were both thankful for his new job. This job paid a little more than his previous job. We had made it over our first financial hurdle. But before I could rejoice, I was facing yet another hurdle. My mother had a very serious mental relapse. This time, however, the hospital would not release her on her own recognizance. They said that she would need someone to care for her because she could no longer live alone. I talked it over with my husband, and we both agreed she should move in with us. He had always been very supportive when it came to my mother. Though we knew it would be challenging, we loved her dearly and she had always been there for us, so we wanted to be there for her. She appeared to be content to know she was returning to live with us, and we welcomed her with outstretched arms.

For Better or For Worse

There was this judge who married us? His questions had come to mind a thousand times over. Do you promise to love him for *richer* or for *poorer,* for *better* or for *worse?* I answered that I would, but I had no idea these things would come so quickly and happen all at once. I had expected the honeymoon to last a little while longer. But then, I guess I was a little naive. We didn't even spend our honeymoon alone because we had to bring our son. It seemed exciting honeymooning on the fish creek with my new husband and son. But somehow it seemed that those moments were fleeting. There is a rhyme we would sing when we were children with the lyrics: "First comes love, then comes marriage" but that is not how it happened with us. Marriage is a very serious undertaking, and God ordained it to be done decent and in order. Due to our ignorance and disobedience, we did things our own way. We had children before we were married.

Some counselors believe that having children before marriage causes problems for newlyweds because they don't have time to talk, share, and learn together. Since we had been together years before we had our first child, we had already learned a lot about each other. Even though we had small children, we always managed to have time to communicate and share. We knew each other quite well and had built a strong relationship before we were married. However, we were saddled with many other obstacles in our first years of marriage. It is good that we had already spent years of getting to know each other because this helped us to keep our marriage intact during our difficult years. Financial woes and the care of relatives were serious issues we encountered during our early years of marriage. It was a blessing we did keep our lines of communication open. When husbands and wives fail to communicate, it places a strain on their relationship. No matter how serious the problem or how difficult the situation was, Calvin and I always found time to talk. Though we did not agree all the time, we would discuss the issues and challenges that seemed to plague our marriage and then come to an agreement.

As we continued to struggle through our first few years of marriage, we took life as it came, learned from our mistakes, and moved on. We definitely had many problems, and most of them stemmed from our finances and family. I believed that if we could just get our finances in order, things would be better. I considered getting a job but my children were small, and I had no one to care for my mother. Be that as it may, we did our best with what we had. My mother would always say, "There is no sense in crying over spilled milk" and I had many tears to shed and lots of milk that had been spilled. There were constant spills; in time, the mop and broom became my constant companions. I was performing all of the duties that were assigned to me as a wife and a mother. I cooked, cleaned, washed, and dried clothes all day long.

Of course, we could not afford a washer and dryer at this time. We had far too many responsibilities: rent, groceries, utilities, gas, baby food, diapers, and more diapers. Did you notice I did not include *tithes*? Yes, I believed in miracles and I believed in God, but I felt that I did not have time to go to church, and I sure didn't have any money to give them or Him. Anyway, at this point in life, shamefully, I must admit that I was so selfishly wrapped up in my own life that I saw God as someone to come to my rescue. I had not spent intimate time with Him for quite some time. I was so busy taking care of a husband and children and managing all of the expenses of running a home that I barely had time for anyone, including myself or God. At that time, I felt that I had too many financial problems of my own to try and help support the church. And during those years, my mother contributed very little to the household budget, as she was on a fixed income. As I stated earlier, my mother only worked as a domestic, so her monthly benefits barely took care of her personal needs. Again, I experienced the mercy of God. Even though during our stressful times we forgot Him, He never forgot us. His word assures us that He will never leave us or forsake us. We tried to be content with the things that we had and just as He promises us in **Hebrews 13:5,** He never left us.

(Now that I think about, it was only after we began to tithe, that our finances have been in order.) I am so thankful that through the word of God and the Holy Spirit guiding us, we finally learned a new way to handle our family and our finances; "Put God first!") **Proverbs 3:9-10**

When we felt like we couldn't last much longer, my husband received another job. We hoped with his new job we would at least be able to have our basic needs met. This was truly a blessing from God and we were grateful. We even started a little savings account. My husband had made great strides on his new job and within the year, he became supervisor and received a large financial increase. God was still blessing us. We began searching for land with hopes of building a home. I couldn't wait to own my own home. Just when I thought things were beginning to take a turn for the better, I felt like "worse" showed up. I started feeling sick every morning and couldn't keep anything on my stomach. When toothpaste made me sick, all doubt was removed and I knew I was pregnant again. I went for the examination just for confirmation and I was right. Another mouth to feed. The baby would be due six months later. My oldest son was almost four years old by then and my youngest was two. When I told my husband, he took it like a champ. "Well, maybe we can even the number out." What? Was he expecting me to have twins? "Three" was an odd number. We only had two sons. We were both excited in spite of our circumstances, and this time, I was sure I would have the little girl I always wanted. Even though our family had grown rather quickly and we were never financially prepared, we never thought of our children as intrusions. Many times, even married couples decide they don't want children and sometimes even choose to abort them, but we saw our children as blessings from God.

Our daughter was born in February. We named her Vallena Vaselle. Ironically in January 1973, a month before she was born, the United States Supreme Court, in a 7 to 2 vote, handed down two rulings legalizing abortions *(Roe vs Wade)*. Since then, millions of babies have been aborted, of course no one really knows, exactly, because there are so many unaccounted. Nevertheless, the discussions and fights continue on.

Over the years, many reasons have been sighted for having abortions such as rape, incest, and abnormality of children. The list goes on and on. I don't know nor can I imagine the place any woman is in at that particular time in her life. Only God knows, and at that point, it then becomes a matter placed in His hands. I do know that I believe life itself is a gift from God. But when I think of abortions, I am saddened not only for the babies, but for the mothers and fathers, also. We sometimes forget that though, we may or may not *always make right choices in life situations, ultimately God is indeed the final judge.* **Jeremiah 17:9-10**

In spite of the outward turmoil, God blessed us with the life of a beautiful daughter who made her appearance during one of the worst snow storms of the South. While I was in the hospital, there were at least eight inches of snow throughout Georgia and other bordering states. I stayed in the hospital three extra days because we were not prepared for this type of weather. It took days for the snow plows to come to our area.

Of course, staying in the hospital for extra days meant more money. My husband had insurance on his new job, but he had an 80/20 plan. The insurance company paid eighty percent of the bill, and we paid the other twenty percent so with our joy came yet another trial. Our lives seemed to always have a mixture of joy and pain all at once. Once we returned home, we had one more addition to our family. The boys were excited to have a little sister, and we all rallied around our new addition. With my mother staying with us, there were now six of us in all. It was obvious we needed a larger place, but we were not sure we could afford it. Buying a home had been put on hold once we had added other responsibilities. I really needed to find a job, but it would cost too much to hire a sitter for three small children, and I still could not leave my mother alone because her mental condition worsened over time.

In time, my husband became overwhelmed by our living conditions so he began to work overtime. He worked late hours, even on the weekends. This was the first time in the twenty years I had known him that I did not feel like we were a team. We continued to drift apart, and I became more withdrawn and stayed inside all day long. The house we lived in was dull and drab. My mother stayed in her room unless she had one of her mental outbursts. My children were all in constant terror of the wild lady with the muzzled hair who would barge out of the room spewing profanity. I began to lose myself in the lives of characters on the daily soap operas. This was my only source of entertainment and the extent of my contact with the rest of the outside world.

As time passed, my mother's condition worsened, and I repeatedly had to take her to stay at the behavioral center for months at a time. I must admit this was a blessing in disguise. God was still there even though I didn't see it at the time. I was able to get a break and clear my mind. After this last episode, before my mother was released from the behavioral center, my husband informed me that we needed to have a serious talk. He told me to contact my siblings and let them know that someone else would have to take my mother into their home. He said we were drifting apart, and we had to get our own house in order. He confessed that he had begun to hang out with single people and that was not good for our marriage. At this point, I was drained, and it was almost too late for me to connect with him. We had drifted so far apart, and I didn't feel as if I knew him anymore. I had come to accept the children screaming, a husband who missed meals, and an erratic mother, as life. I had become detached from everyone and was comfortable just staying in my room feeling sorry for myself. I only interacted with my children and that was because of my duty as a mother.

I now realize that I was probably in a state of depression and didn't even know it. Psychologists say over one half of the people who are depressed are really unaware of it, and I can safely say that I was one of those people. I managed to muster up enough energy to call my siblings. My older brother agreed to take my mother into his home. He was remarried by this time, but his new wife took her in. I knew this would be a challenge for his family as well, so I was especially grateful to him since I always felt that our mother was my responsibility. Many times, families have to take on the responsibility of caring for a parent or other family member. This was true throughout the years and today it is no different. Even now, more husbands and wives are taking care of their parents because people are living longer. In some cases, the added responsibility of taking care of parents has caused serious problems between spouses and sometimes even leads to divorce. I was grateful that our situation did not end that way. But I must admit, at times, we came very close to it.

During the 1970's, according to U.S. statistics, divorce rates tripled. I remember hearing the phrases "no fault divorce" and "irreconcilable differences." My generation was called the "Baby Boomers" and that we were. I think we were a generation of new birth and change. We had a new attitude about life. "Live and Let Live" and "Do Your Own Thing" were some of the mottos of the day. Nevertheless, I had always believed that marriage was forever and in spite of the many challenges we encountered, my husband and I managed to work out our differences. In 2023, United States continues to see complex trends in divorce rates, with an overall decline, according to most statistics. I also read that *Baby Boomers* (like us), have the highest divorce rate among our current generations of marriage.

I am thankful that during very challenging times we were able to still maintain our marriage. I am also grateful that we had my brother's help and other family members to care for my mother. Afterwards, we moved from our little shabby home into a cute little house on the other side of town. My husband called it our "Little Matchbox." Things did get much better for our family. Our new place was not in a dark alley and the neighborhood was very pleasant. It had a big yard where the children enjoyed playing outside. They could even ride their bikes on the outside around the house. My husband came home a lot more, and we were the happiest we had ever been as a family. However, the children seemed to recover and adjust a lot faster than I did. It took me almost a year to get out of the habit of just sitting in the living room watching soap operas. I started taking the children outside and playing games with them. In the past, they had stayed inside most of the day watching television, but now I knew I needed to do more, if nothing else, for them.

During this time my mother-in-law became ill and moved in with us for a while. We had some great times and were able to enjoy, go on some fun trips before she passed. She was a woman full of faith, through it all. She went to stay with her children up north, before she passed away, a few years, later.

Indeed, time is filled with swift transition. A year after my mother-in-law passed, my husband's sister passed away. Of course, none of us saw this coming and to add to all of this, I was now pregnant with our fourth child. Shortly after the funeral, I gave birth to another girl. We named her Fredena Ozia Ezell after her grandmother, grandfather, and her aunt. Again, we experienced yet another bittersweet moment. As I rejoiced in the birth of our daughter, I was also saddened that her grandmother and aunt would not get to meet her. I had an easy pregnancy and the baby came quickly. I always counted it as a blessing that I did not have to stay in labor for long hours when giving birth to my children. We now had four children. It was then that I understood what my husband meant when he said we could even things out. He told me he had always prayed and planned to have *four* children. He wanted two boys and two girls. Now that we had evened things out our nest was complete.

After a while, the joy finally began to come back after having been dealt such devastating blow from losing his mother and sister, and my in-laws. With God's comfort again, I felt much better about myself and our lives. Isn't that just how it is? We all have our ups and downs, but if we can get through them, we can enjoy the blessings of God in spite of the pain. *James 1:2-4* I heard someone say that the one thing about life is that you can always depend on it to change, good or bad. So, it is very important to enjoy life while you can.

In Sickness and In Health

Yes! It is important to enjoy and embrace life while you can because life does not always remain the same. Life always changes. For years, my family had experienced many changes and faced many challenges in our lives, but this time it really changed for the worse. Now, it appeared that after fifteen years of marriage and what seemed like the healthiest time in our marriage, sickness showed up. Again, I thought of my marital vows. Do you promise to love him in sickness and in health? We had nursed a few aches and pains, colds and flu over the years of our marriage, but what we faced next was something more serious. It had been eight years since the birth of our last child and we were enjoying life. For some reason though, I felt an uneasiness, as if something just wasn't right.

It started when my husband began to go to bed late. He made sure he always climbed in bed after I did. He seemed distant and appeared to have something on his mind, but he did not share. This was quite unusual, but I tried to give him space. Surely, he would share with me soon. One evening, when he quietly retreated into our bedroom, I followed him. He was taking off his shirt and what I saw startled me. I saw a large lump on his back. I stood frozen in my tracks with my hand over my mouth. At first, I was speechless. I then shouted, "Oh, My God!" He turned around and softly said, "It's alright." His secret had been revealed. I sat on the edge of bed feeling numb and lifeless. I couldn't move. I wanted to question him, but instead I finally stood up and left the room. How had he hidden this? I needed time alone with God. Somewhere between all of the babies, bottles, and battles of life I had neglected my relationship with God. That night I found a quiet place to read and commune with God. I needed God's strength and His direction. I prayed and asked Him to give me strength and guidance through His son Jesus Christ. I needed to find a physician and it couldn't wait.

I was glad my mother had taken me to Sunday school and church. There is a scripture that tells us to: *"Train up a child in the way that he should go and he will not depart from it"* **Proverbs 22:6.** I had been taught to pray to God. I had been told to read the scriptures. Though I had prayed to God throughout my trials and tribulations, I had never searched the scriptures for answers. But this time, I remembered and opened my Bible and began not only to read, but to search the scriptures for wisdom, knowledge, healing, power, and peace. I knew I had to remain calm and have peace in order to carry on. I picked up the phone book, and I began to search the yellow pages for a physician. I spent hours searching for a physician and days of reading God's Word and praying for direction.

While reading the Bible, one night I was led to read two passages of scripture. One was **Romans 11** and the other was **II Kings 20.** I read them over and over with very little understanding. Though I did not totally understand, I knew God was speaking to me through those verses. **Romans 11:16** stated: *"If the first fruit is holy, the lump is holy, and if the root is holy, so are the branches."* The other scripture in **II Kings 20** told of a great King named Hezekiah who had a sickness. Hezekiah had a "lump" (boil) and he asked God not to let him die and God heard his prayer and added fifteen more years to his life. What did this mean to me and my situation? I had no idea.

I was so grateful that I had begun to read the scriptures. I don't know what I would have done without them. I am sure God knew I would need His Word during these trying times. In His Word, I found peace and strength. My faith was renewed with each passing day. Through His Word, He had been preparing me for the worst, while strengthening me for the months ahead. God is omniscient, for He is indeed an all knowing and awesome God.

Faith in a Fig?

For the next few days, I stayed in prayer. I took a few days off from work to process the things that had taken place. After my children got older, I was successful at finding a job outside of the home and all was well until now. I had a lot of questions racing through my mind but no answers. What was God saying? What were the scriptures I read saying to me? What was God's Word telling me? What was my husband's state of mind? I had so many questions that needed answers.

One thing I did know was that my husband did not want a biopsy. He was adamant about that. I did not understand why, but I knew I had to find a way to respect his wishes. But how could we find out anything without having a biopsy? There was no doubt in my mind. I knew the "lump" had to be removed and tested, but I didn't know how. It seemed impossible without a biopsy, but I truly believed that all things are possible with God. So, once again, I needed a miracle. I continued to pray. Over the past years, God had shown me that through our faith in Him, He hears our prayers and He always answers them in one way or the other. *Romans 8:26-28*

That night, after seeing the lump on my husband's back, I continued to read my Bible and meditate on His Word. I was led back to the verses in chapter *20 of II Kings*. I read the scripture of how God sent word to King Hezekiah, telling him to place a "lump of figs" on his back and he would be healed. I remember thinking, Lord we have some figs. Since we have a fig tree in our backyard, I got up and went to the tree and pulled three figs. I remember the year was 1986, and it was the middle of June. The figs on the tree had not ripened, so they were still green. I went outside and pulled three green figs. I went back inside and asked my husband if I could place them on his back. He said that it couldn't hurt. In faith, I pressed the three green figs over the lump on his back and I cried out to God. I remember praying and seeing the white milky substance oozing down my husband's back. I prayed, "Lord if you healed Hezekiah, I know you can heal my husband." Nothing happened, or so I thought.

After the itching stopped, my husband went outside to play basketball with the boys while the girls and I were the cheerleaders. In our backyard, at the old fig tree, we had a makeshift basketball court. My younger son threw the basketball to my eldest son who went up for a jump shot. He made the basket and as he came down, he fell on my husband's back. My husband looked at me and said, "Well it's off." He ended the game abruptly, and we went inside. When he pulled up his shirt, the lump was hanging loosely by a thin thread of tissue. I rushed to the linen closet, grabbed a towel and gave it to him so he could hold the lump in place. I called the kids inside and told them we had to go to the hospital, which was about thirty miles away. It is amazing how none of us panicked. It had to be the peace of God for which I had prayed. I don't even remember the children asking a lot of questions. They were given instructions to remain at home in the care of our oldest son.

As soon as we arrived to the hospital, the receptionist began to take my husband's information. When we showed her, the lump hanging off, she rushed us to the back. The physician came in, looked at the lump, and asked us what happened. It was clear he was surprised by what he saw. When we told him, the lump had been "knocked" off, he asked if there was any blood. We showed him the towel and watched him as he studied it curiously. He was looking for another towel with more blood, but there wasn't one. We told him that was it. There were only three drops of blood on the towel. The physician was amazed and kept saying that my husband should be bleeding but there was no blood. The lump appeared to have been carefully removed by a surgeon. All the physician did was snip the little tissue and place a covering over the area. He placed the "lump" in a bag. He sent it to the hospital lab and told us the wound could possibly begin to bleed in the night. If it should, we were to return to the emergency room. It never bled.

At checkout, the nurse told us we would hear from an oncologist within three days. From that statement, we assumed that they suspected the lump was cancerous. We left the office in faith, knowing God had already performed a miracle. Who would believe that God had removed the lump on my husband's back, using our own backyard as the operating room, our eldest son as the surgeon, and a basketball as the surgical instrument? *There was no anesthesia given.*

As I left the hospital, I was reminded of another operation that took place in a beautiful backyard where the Garden of Eden was a *"hospital"* where God miraculously performed surgery without anesthesia. The story in the second book of Genesis reads: *"And the Lord God caused a deep sleep to fall on Adam, and he slept; and He took one of his ribs, and closed up the flesh in its place. Then the rib which the Lord God had taken from man, He made into a woman, and He brought her to the man". And Adam said: This is now bone of my bones and flesh of my flesh; She shall be called Woman because she was taken out of Man"* **Genesis 2:21-23.** *Behold, I am the God of all flesh. Is there anything too hard for me?* **Jeremiah 32:27**

Before going to bed that night, I thanked God for all of His many blessings. *I was thankful that his miracles were not only of old but for yesterday, today, and forever!* **Hebrews 13:8** I truly believed that if He removed the lump, He would heal the wound. My faith was not in the *fig* but my faith was in Him.

My faith was in God and I believed then and now that God does not only heal kings and rulers, but ordinary people, like you and me. God is no respecter of persons **Acts 10:34.** If we just have faith and believe in His Son Jesus Christ, there is nothing too hard for Him. With men this is impossible, but with God all things are possible. **Matthew 19:26**

Lord, You Send Me a Jew

I waited anxiously to receive the lab results from the hospital and a call from the oncologist. After almost a week, I heard nothing. However, at the end of the week, I got a call that the lab results were in, and my husband had been referred to a local oncologist. Because of the urgency, the physician scheduled an emergency appointment for the next morning. After examining my husband, the specialist told him he needed surgery immediately. The oncologist wanted to set him up for surgery the same day; however, we told him we would give him a call within a few days. We definitely needed to hear from God. Before the end of the week, we received a letter in the mail from the oncologist. The letter was blunt and very unprofessional. The physician simply stated that if my husband did not have surgery soon, he would be dead. The next letter said, *"Don't wait too long!"* After receiving these letters in the mail, we knew this was not the surgeon for us.

The next day, I sat down, collected myself and redirected my thoughts to the situation at hand. My husband needed a surgeon, and I wanted to find the best in the land. And surely, the specialist the hospital referred was not the one. I prayed to the Lord and asked for a surgeon. As I prayed, the scripture from Romans 11 flashed across my mind. That particular scripture not only referred to the "lump" being holy, but it also gave insight about God's chosen people and their restoration. I read about others being grafted in with God's chosen people. As I continued to pray, I found myself not only asking God to send a surgeon but to let him be a Jew. Where did that come from? To my knowledge, I didn't know a single Jew. At that particular time, I did not read the Old Testament very often. My focus had primarily been the New Testament. Therefore, I did not understand the fullness of God's purpose for all of His people especially the Israelites. I did not understand why God chose Israel. Since that time, I have come to know and understand that God as our Creator, has the right to do whatever he chooses and to choose whomever He so pleases. And for His own purpose, He chose Israel as His "special people." *I Peter 2:9-10*

Jews were purposely intertwined in His eternal and everlasting plan for His people. When I hear evangelists, prophets, and pastors herald the blessedness of God's promises to Israel, I feel blessed just to know that since I accepted Christ, I have been grafted in. I pray for the peace of Jerusalem and that America will bless and be a blessing to Israel, so she too can be blessed. Through the scripture, I knew God was giving me bits and pieces of information about a Jewish physician. God truly speaks to us through His Word if we have a personal relationship with Him through His Son Jesus Christ. I was sure He was sending me to a Jew, even though I didn't know where to find one. I should have known that God Himself could find a Jew. After all, He found Nathaniel the Israelite under a fig tree *John 1:48*. I was confident that somewhere out in the world, there was a Jew just waiting to bless us.

For some reason, I kept thinking about my aunt and uncle's daughter, *Lola* who was a nurse in Atlanta. I decided to call her thinking that maybe she knew a good surgeon, and just as I had hoped, she did. After I told her about my husband's condition, she recommended a surgeon. I called and scheduled an appointment the next day and was thankful they were able to fit us in. Normally, you need referrals and it takes weeks, sometimes months. But thanks be to God, a door was opened. Someone had cancelled and the specialist did not even ask for a referral.

On the day of the appointment, I drove my husband over one hundred miles to the physician's office. Since my cousin had told us that this surgeon was the best, I didn't mind the drive. We arrived safely and the drive was not bad. When we walked into the office, I felt amazingly calm. We laughed and chatted until the physician called us in. As far as I could tell, he was not a Jew. He was a young

African-American man who had studied hard, graduated from medical school, and then moved to the city to start his own practice. He had done well over the years and enjoyed his work. He also told us he had been raised about one hundred miles south of our hometown. I was later informed that he was listed as one of the top physicians in America and around the world. I was impressed and so was my husband. Though, he was not the Jew for whom I prayed, we felt very comfortable with him.

Once the formalities were out of the way, he got down to business. After the examination, he decided that my husband's illness was somewhat complicated, and he would refer him to another physician who was not only an oncologist but also performed reconstructive surgery. He highly recommended this physician. He called ahead to see if the specialist could schedule us in, and he did. We checked out at the front desk and went across the walkway to the oncologist who also performed reconstructive surgery. Sometimes, God has to send us to more than one person to get us to the place He wants us to go. It was a very short walk to the physician's office. As soon as we entered the office, the nurse called us in. The receptionist allowed us to complete our paperwork after the examination. Oh! But for the favor of God!

As we entered the examination room, my eyes quickly focused on a picture of a young boy at a Bar Mitzvah. There were pictures of several trips to the Holy Land, along with all kinds of Jewish celebrations. Could it be that this surgeon was a Jew? The physician walked in as I was admiring his pictures. His voice was proud as he told us he had just returned from the *Holy Land*. I could tell he was full of excitement. Before he began to examine my husband, he gave us all of the details of his trips to the Holy Land. Israel was his homeland, and he visited Israel at least once a year. I was overjoyed that God had sent me to the Jew for whom I had prayed. We were in awe as we listened to all of his stories about his trip. I was speechless. At that very moment, I knew God had sent us to His chosen surgeon with the hands which He would use. Since that time, in 2016, I had the opportunity to visit the Holy Land. Oh! what a blessing! I am reminded of God's Word: *"Thus says the LORD of hosts: In those days ten men from every language of the nations shall grasp the sleeve of a Jewish man, saying, "Let us go with you, for we have heard that God is with you." Zechariah 8:23*

The Examination

As the physician finished telling us about his trip to the Holy Land, he handed my husband a patient's gown and left the room. When he returned, he pulled up his chair and asked a very unique and unusual question: *"What's your story?"* Usually, physicians ask questions like: What seems to be the problem? Or why are you here? I always chuckle on the inside when a physicians asks those questions. But this doctor surprised us with his question. I guess he noticed the quizzical look on our faces, so he just said, "Well, I know someone has been praying." *How did he know that?* But he was right. Both my husband and I had been praying continually and seeking God's direction as we searched for a surgeon.

We all sat quietly for a few minutes, then I began to speak first. As I began to tell him our story about the lump, the figs, and the incident with the basketball and our trip to the emergency room, I could see that he was both spiritually and medically intrigued. Even as I spoke, I was thanking God in my spirit for answering my prayer. There was such peace in the room, and I knew it was the presence of the Lord. I was in awe at how God had orchestrated this meeting. He knew exactly where to find the *"Jew"* who had everything we needed. He was not only an oncologist but also a reconstructive surgeon. He knew the surgeon's heart and the gifts he had planted within him. <u>What a mighty God!</u>

After I finished talking, the physicians told us he was going to take care of my husband. I remember he told him when he finished with him, he would be "as good as new." He examined my husband thoroughly before describing his illness in detail. He recommended surgery. If the lump was cancerous, a large area of the back would have to be removed and it would leave a rather large hole in the center of my husband's back. This was the reason reconstructive surgery was needed. It was indeed critical. My husband would need two surgeries. One to remove the lump and one to restore the area. The surgeon would have to do a skin graft. That was a very familiar word since I had been reading about it in Romans 11 for over a month. He told us that skin grafting was very tedious. The surgeon would take skin from one area of the body and use it to cover the hole in my husband's back. It was very important that the skin graft was successful on the first try; therefore, a nurse would be assigned to actually sit at my husband's bedside for many hours and actually hold the graft in place. If this was done incorrectly, the whole process would have to be repeated. There was no way I was going to allow that to happen so I asked the physicians if I could do it. Surprisingly, he agreed and asked if I was "up for the challenge". I hesitated, but I knew God would strengthen me. *Philippians 4:13,* I knew that I wanted the graft to take more than anyone else, so I would lovingly persevere.

Before we left the office, the physicians told us there was a man who had an appointment change and had come in early. This man had the exact surgery done a few years ago. His surgery was a success. The physicians asked if we wanted to see the results of the surgery, and of course, we did. He went out and asked the patient, and thankfully, he agreed. There before us was an amazingly beautiful skin graft. That might sound peculiar, but to see it, you knew no one could have done it but God. It was amazing how God created the body in such a way that it could heal itself. After we thanked the gentlemen for his kindness and encouragement, he returned back to the waiting room. God had orchestrated yet another "divine encounter" so we could not only *"believe"* but we could *"believe and know"* that all things are possible through Him, and if we ask anything anything in confidence according to His will, He hears us. *I John 5:13-15*

After the gentlemen left the room, the oncologist began to give us more words of encouragement. He told us he would send all of his reports and results to the Armed Institute of Pathology. He had the records from the results of the biopsy sent to the Armed Forces Institute of Pathology because he was concerned that the tumor could have come from contact with harmful chemicals. Since my husband was on an ammunition ship that transported chemicals and ammunition, he immediately sent the tissue to them as well.

We returned home the same day and waited patiently for a call from the surgeon with the lab results. We were thoroughly convinced that God was in control of every aspect of my husband's illness. In spite of the circumstances, I left the surgeon's office with a peace that passed all understanding. Truly, my soul was waiting on God, and my expectation was of Him *Psalm 62:5.*

While we were dealing with my husband's illness, I was working outside of the home. I enjoyed my new experience. My aunt and uncle watched the children after school. My uncle was retired by now and this gave them a little extra income. My mother had been mentally stable for a few years and was able to live alone. Since my aunt and uncle were on the next street from my mother, they kept a close watch over her also. We had moved back to our old neighborhood to be close to our family, so we had additional help for our children while I was at work. Though I had not worked steadily for years, surprisingly, I was hired by a very large corporation. I had tried working for short periods of time in between pregnancies, but it never worked out because of babysitting needs and my mother's illness. But I guess these odd jobs plus my earlier past work experience were enough to obtain the job. I was hired as an invoice clerk in the accounting department.

Since I was working, I gave the receptionist my work number. When I received the phone call at work, I was surprised when the call was from someone other than the receptionist. The caller identified himself as a pathologist from the Armed Forces Institute of Pathology. He said he was calling me himself because he had the results of my husband's lab tests. The results were not good. He said he was sorry to inform me that the results showed my husband only had three months to live. It felt like every sound around me was silenced by his words. My heart sank.

I could hear the voice on the other end calling me. "Ma'am, are you still there? Are you alright?" I guess he had expected a loud scream or something, but I found myself just gripping the phone. Finally, I mustered up the strength to answer him. "Yes, thank you, Sir. I will make an appointment with his physician." I really don't remember much after that. I just dropped the phone and started screaming the words three months over and over. My coworker came over and I could barely tell her what happened. After they heard the screams, my supervisor and several other people had come into the office. My supervisor took me into her office and helped me to calm down. After I calmed down enough to explain what happened, she allowed my friend *(Val)* to drive me home. We carpooled every day. It was a thirty-minute commute.

During the drive, I spent most of those thirty minutes trying to imagine my life without my husband. We had four children who I did not want to have to raise alone. What would I tell them? How would I break the news to him? This was another one of those times when I wanted to cry but couldn't. I began praying and talking to God. My mind flashed back to the scripture in II Kings. I remember King Hezekiah had asked God not to let him die, and God added fifteen more years to his life. I prayed, "O Lord God, you did it for King Hezekiah, please do it for me and my children. You removed the lump, now save his life."

It seemed as though the thirty-minute drive took hours. As soon as I entered the house, my phone was ringing. I missed it. A few minutes later, my coworker Vickie called and told me I had received another call from The Armed Institute of Pathology. I was to call them immediately. She gave me the number. When I called the pathologist on site, I was told they had somehow misread the results. Even though my husband's illness was critical, they believed that with surgery, he could possibly recover. God heard our prayers. I couldn't wait to give my husband the good news. It was not the best news, but it was much better than having to tell him he only had three months to live. I explained to him the situation with the mix-up of the lab results (so they said), but we knew it was God. We were both grateful we still had time together to raise our children, but we knew we had to prepare ourselves for the months ahead. We would now have to wait patiently for the call from the oncologist to set up the date for surgery. Nevertheless, we were confident that God would be with us as always during these most trying times.

Gifted Hands

The following week, we received a call from the oncologist. He had talked with the Institute, and they had diagnosed my husband with a *Bednar Fibro Sarcoma Tumor*. He apologized for the mix up at the lab and assured us that the surgery would go well. He told us the surgery needed to be set up immediately because of the chances of infection in the open wound. We had two weeks to get everything in order. We had a lot of planning to do in a very short time. I had to train a temporary person on my job, and I also had to make arrangements for someone to care for the children. My husband and I spent a lot of time in prayer, thanking God and reminiscing over our lives. When you are faced with critical illnesses, somehow it makes you appreciate life even more. When we received our pre-op papers in the mail, they were very frightening. There is always a statement that lets you know there is a chance of mishaps beyond the physician's control. We were thankful we knew God and that we put our trust in Him. *Psalm 31:14* We were told we would probably have to stay at the hospital for ten days. We had already contacted our close relatives and friends about the seriousness of the surgery for we knew we would need their love and support.

However, we did not give our children all of the details. We only told them that their father had to have surgery in Atlanta and that my mother, aunt, and uncle would be taking care of them. I was glad my mother was stable at this most critical time in our lives. Looking back, there were some times that God seemed to work it out that way. Of course, some of my other family members had agreed to help out as well. We assured the children that God would be with all of us. We had begun to take them to Sunday school and church, so we were confident they understood. By now, they were all teenagers, except our youngest daughter who was only eight years old. The boys were sixteen and fourteen, and our oldest daughter was thirteen. We told them that we were depending on them to take care of their little sister, and they did.

On the day before surgery, we traveled to the city at *West Paces Ferry Hospital,* in Atlanta, (which is now closed) to make certain Calvin was able to get some rest. The time seemed to rush by, and in what seemed like only a moment, we were at the hospital for surgery. We arrived early for check in, and they began the routine prep work. Afterwards, they took my husband in for surgery. As they wheeled him out of the room, I followed them to the elevator. As the elevator door began to close, he managed a smile and gave me a *"thumbs up."* He had been sedated but was not completely out of it.

I had a very long wait, especially since I was alone. I had told my family that I would rather them stay at home and take care of the children. I don't know why, but somehow, I felt better being alone. This time, the time moved in slow motion. I tried to occupy my mind with thoughts of our family and prayers for our strength. Some of the time was occupied by the nurse, who had been given very specific instructions by the physician to teach me what I needed to do. Finally, six hours later, the physician came to the room with a wide smile on his face and told me all was well. I would get to see my husband after his stay in recovery. Now it was my turn. I had prepared my heart and mind to do my part. The graft was equally as important as the surgery, and I was prepared to do what I needed to do. I was a little nervous, but I knew with God's help I could do it. I was thankful that I had learned about God and come to an understanding of His Son Jesus Christ just in time. Otherwise, I don't know how I would have made it through this entire ordeal.

When I arrived at the nurse's station, a fun-loving nurse was waiting for me. She introduced herself and asked me to follow her. She had a "basket of goodies" which included heavy stuffed gauze patches, tape, antiseptics, petroleum jelly, and other tubes of ointments. The nurse began to show me the procedure and technique I was to use. She gave me a few encouraging words, then continued with her daily duties. The wait seemed forever, but soon they brought my husband to his assigned room. I thought he would be drowsy, but he was very alert and in his usual happy mood. Shortly afterwards, the nurse came in to show me my first holding position. It wasn't so bad once I got the hang of it. I had to sit for many hours for two days praying and carefully holding the gauze and the graft in place. Whenever I had to leave, I would have to call a nurse to take my place. I made as few trips as possible because I wanted to make sure the skin graft was successful the first time, and I believed I had been given the strength necessary to make this happen.

After a few days, the physician informed us the graft was beautifully done. He even brought other physicians and interns from the local medical school and university at *Emory* to admire our work. He said he had never seen anything so beautiful. Of all of the skin grafts he had ever done; he proclaimed this one to be his greatest work. He praised me for a job well done. *To God be the glory*! I knew that without Him, I could not have persevered. I knew that there were still more challenges ahead, but I was thankful that the surgery had gone so well.

My husband was dismissed after seven days. We chose not to use an ambulatory service back home; instead, we drove our car. The ride was very challenging, and we had to make several stops. It was difficult for my husband to get comfortable and of course, I did not want to risk any injuries while we were driving. As we traveled, we discussed our plans for the coming months. We believed we had been given the gift of many more years of happiness together. I knew without doubt God had answered all of our prayers. I was confident that just as He had added fifteen more years to King Hezekiah's life, he would add even more years to my husband's life. For His Word is truth and He is able to do exceedingly and abundantly above all that we ask or think, according to the power that works in us **Ephesians 3:20.** Some *thirty-seven* (37) years later, His promise was fulfilled above and beyond all measure, and for this, we can never thank Him enough.

Again, I remembered **Romans 11** and reflected upon **verse 23**: *"And if they do not persist in unbelief, they will be grafted in, for God is able to graft them in, again."* Now I understood what God was saying before. If the lump was removed and we believed in Him, He had the power to graft it in again. He could repair and restore and He did it simply by using the gifted hands of a "chosen" Jew and a "lowly" Gentile *like me.*

The amazing thing is this! My husband never had chemotherapy or radiation before or afterwards. He just went for annual check-ups for 3 years. Only God!

"For I will restore health to you and heal you of your wounds, says the Lord."

Jeremiah 30:17

Do It Again, Lord

We were excited to leave the hospital so we could get home to see our children. Several of our family members were there when we arrived. It looked as if the children had grown while we were away. We were all happy to be together again. I cannot recall a time when we had ever been apart that long. Although our children were excited to see both of us, they rallied around their father. I had to monitor them to keep them from touching his wound. The children knew their father was ill, but they never knew the full extent of his illness.

It took days for them to recall all of the activities that had taken place while we were away. But all in all, things went quite well. We had lost part of our income, but life moves on and we had to get back into the swing of things. A few years before his illness, my husband had gone into business. We tried to keep the paint business moving during his stay in the hospital by having some of our friends and family members pitch in to carry the load. Once we returned, everything was still intact. In spite of our bout with illness, life was good. My job paid well and it helped to defray the costs of running a business. Since it was a job with a major corporation, the benefits were excellent. With a self-employed husband and four children, these benefits were very much needed. Private healthcare for a small business owner was practically unaffordable. It is interesting how more than *thirty-five* (35) years later, the nation is still having healthcare issues, in spite of what was called healthcare reforms, healthcare costs are still skyrocketing in the United States.

Nevertheless, I was especially thankful for my healthcare benefits in the nineties, because they paid all of my husband's medical expenses. However, I did not know that I would need these same benefits a few years later. Surprisingly, I would have an on-the-job injury caused by simply sitting at a computer. I was an invoice clerk, so I sat at a desk all day, which many would consider a non-hazardous job. Sometimes, I worked as many as twelve hours. Unfortunately, the uncomfortable chair that I sat in was high while the desk was extremely low. I sat with my head down and my neck bent all day long. Over the years, I began to experience weakness in my neck and arms. It became so severe that every day after work, I would go home and go straight to bed. Once in bed, I could only sleep in a fetal position. The pain was constant and neither time nor medicine seemed to help.

One day while sitting in a twelve-hour workshop, I passed out. I was sitting in the chair, and I was told that I just fell backward. The company nurse examined me, and she concluded that it was just exhaustion. They ordered me to take leave for a few days and get some rest. Nevertheless, in spite of rest, the symptoms continued. Even a task as simple as getting out of the bed became too much for me. I returned to the physician, but they found nothing. Finally, I had to take extended sick leave. I knew that I had to do something, but I just did not know what to do. During this time in my life, I was referred to sixteen different specialists with no concrete diagnosis. I went to gynecologists, urologists, and neurologist, just to name a few. I had X-rays and CT scans of my neck, head, and back, and through it all, I had no one to turn to but God.

As I was reading a magazine one day, I stumbled across an article that discussed an illness called RSI (Repetitive Stress Injury). I had never heard of this illness, but it carried all of the symptoms that were plaguing my body. *I was so excited!* It may seem ridiculous to become excited about having symptoms of a certain illness, but since no one could diagnose me, I was relieved to have evidence of what I had been experiencing. Many of the specialists attempted to convince me that the symptoms were "in my mind". Even my family had become skeptical and labeled me a hypochondriac. Even now, I still cannot understand why it took so long for the diagnosis. Only God knows!

Since I had been away from work for months without diagnosis, the company asked if I would agree to see a psychiatrist. If I refused to seek psychiatric care, I would have to return to work. As ridiculous, as I thought this was, I agreed to take medical leave for reasons of mental stress instead of physical illness. I did not like this, but I had no choice. I could no longer sit at the desk for long periods of time because the pain was so severe. I also had to apply for workmen's compensation since this appeared to be an on-the-job injury, but when I called the Workmen's Compensation Board, they told me it would best if I had legal representation. I did not understand their request since the board was supposed to be the employee's advocate, but upon the recommendation of a friend, I sought an attorney in the local area. He told me I had a very good case and accepted it on *contingency,* meaning I did not have to pay for legal services until after I received my settlement.

Because of several postponements that were out of my control, the court process took much longer than I had anticipated. Finally, the day came for my trial date, and I was anxious to get the case over with. I was physically and emotionally drained. It seemed like we had only been given a brief reprieve from my husband's illness before I entered my own, and the experiences with hospitals and doctors had taken its toll. When I walked into the courtroom, I was relieved this was finally over and I would be getting the help I needed very soon. However, little did I know that it was just the beginning. When I went to court, there was a very short hearing to establish my name, address, and the makings of my case. I had several witnesses, but only one was called, and she was asked two questions: her name and how long we had worked together. Minutes later, I was told we would have to have another hearing.

As I waited for my next hearing, my funds continued to dwindle and I became restless. All I wanted was compensation so that I would not have to suffer at that desk any longer. At this time, I did not receive workmen's compensation or disability. Though I had paid into the company disability plan, I could not receive disability because I had to file for workmen's compensation and my workmen's compensation claim was tied up within the court system. I was in a "catch-22". At this point, all of our household bills were overdue and we were on the brink of losing everything.

As a last resort, I went to the state to get assistance but was told that I had too many assets. I would have to sell everything I owned before I could get any assistance. Ludicrous! Since this was the way, the system was set up, I knew that this was another situation where all we could do was trust God and hope for the best. I could tell this was going to be yet another long and difficult time for us.

After many more weeks of struggling financially, I received a call from my job to schedule an appointment with the company physician. There, I was given multiple tests that did not reveal anything. After a series of other physicians and tests, I finally received a breakthrough when the company referred me back to my family physician who, in turn, recommended me to a specialist). This *neurologist* ordered an EMG (Electromyogram), which is a nerve induction test. During the test, I felt small electric shocks throughout my body. Unlike the other physicians, he seemed determined to find the cause of my pain. He was also very comforting. I knew he was a godsend. He told me I had suffered for a long time, and *he was going to get me well.* He reminded me of the surgeon whom God had led us to, during my husband's illness. I cried because this was the first time a physician had said these words to me. Much to my surprise, he too was a *Jew* and this time I had not prayed for one. These were the same words that the oncologist had spoken to my husband. I was reminded of God's Word in **Matthew 6:8** which tells us that God knows what we have need of before we even ask.

After my examination, I was referred to a neurosurgeon). I had an overnight hospital stay, and was given an MRI (Magnetic Resonance Imaging) and a Myelogram. The results were astonishing. I needed surgery right away. The physician told me I had a neck that "looked twice its age" (*82 yrs.*). He explained every detail of the process. Ironically, just as my husband had, I would need two surgeries. I would have to have an orthopedic specialist to take a bone from my hip and a neurosurgeon to place it in my neck. This is called *a cervical fusion.* Since the damaged discs were in my upper neck and near my brain, the surgery would be critical. There was a fifty percent chance that I would become paralyzed afterwards, and a fifty percent chance that I would die during this operation. Or, I could live and have God make me whole again, and this is what I chose. I had been in constant pain for six years and survived. I had come to know that with God's help, I would make it through this illness. I had already seen His miraculous power at work through my husband's illness. If He did it once, I knew without a doubt, *"He could do it, again."*

Near Death Experience?

I had to wait six weeks before I could have surgery. Since I had been under the care of so many physicians and had multiple tests, the physicians had to review and compile all of the information. After experiencing the wait of my husband's test results, I was less anxious this time. I had learned to wait patiently and trust in God. I knew that my surgery would take place at the appointed time and that God was in control. Not only that, I had learned to glory in my tribulations. ***Romans 5:3*** As I entered the hospital on the day of surgery, I felt an unspeakable joy and a spirit of peace. As I was taken to the operating room, I was less nervous. I did not have to pray for strength because it was already carrying me down the halls, onto the elevator, and finally through the doors into the cold operating room. I could faintly hear the gentlemen who was pushing my bed ask me why I had such a big smile. He chuckled and told me I acted as though he was pushing me to a grand hotel room instead of an operating room. He was exactly right. I was sick, but I still felt joy in my heart. Even though I was on my way to the operating room, I had no fear, only hope. Then, I remembered being in a very cold room lying on a table looking up at masks with eyes staring down at me.

My surgery had been scheduled to last five and half hours; however, it only lasted three and a half. The physician told me it was a blessing that I had very little "fatty tissue." Up until now my weight fluctuated, usually I weighed less than one hundred and thirty pounds. Now, I am truly glad that my surgery was over *thirty-three* (33) years ago. The physician surely could not have made that comment today because now at age *seventy-four* (74), I have even more *"fatty tissue."* And my weight does not fluctuate, it just continues to increase! As a result of my size, back then, my surgery ended sooner than expected, and also this probably helped it to go extremely well. After surgery that day, I only stayed in recovery for a few hours. My husband was waiting for me in the room to which I was assigned. Within a few days, all of the intravenous tubes were removed and I was preparing to go home soon.

That evening, the physician came in and told me he was going on vacation and needed to examine me before he left. He told me that I could go home the next day. I was excited and my husband began packing my bags. Everything was going well until around 2:00, the next morning. I was awakened out of a very comfortable sleep and remember looking at giant illuminated numbers on the face of the clock. My husband had brought our alarm clock from home. He spent the night with me and had to get up early and dress for work. As I looked at the big green numbers on the clock, I could feel the room spinning. *I tried to get up to use the restroom but each time I raised up, I fell backward onto the bed. I tried again; however, I felt as though someone pushed me back down.* I saw my husband asleep on the chair next to my bed. He seemed lifeless. I repeatedly called his name, but he could not hear me. Though I felt that I was screaming as loud as I could, it seemed as though the words from my mouth were barely above a whisper. I kept reaching for the buzzer and couldn't grab it because my husband had wrapped the cord neatly around the buzzer.

Many people tell stories of having a *"near death"* experience. Many of them say they saw a bright light. Well, so did I. They say they saw a tunnel. Some even say that they saw their loved ones who have passed away. I saw all of these things. While my head was spinning, I saw my grandmother who had died a few years before. I began calling out to her, "Big Mama! Oh, Big Mama!" I continued to cry out, "Big Mama, help me! Jesus save me! I don't want to die! My baby is only 12 years old!" She was standing far away in the middle of a beam of light. I cried out to her, but she never came to me. The light was so bright that I could not look directly at it. Finally, it just faded away. *I felt my body being lifted as my head was spinning at a tremendous amount of speed. Then, it was as if I had a quick drop. It was the strangest feeling I had ever felt in my life.*

Somehow, I finally reached the buzzer. I hit the buzzer long and hard. No one came. I managed to hit it again. This time, the nurses came rushing into my room. They took my vital signs and began hooking me up to intravenous fluids. The nurses called a *"Code Blue"*. All of my vital signs were out of normal range and the attendants worked fervently to figure out what was happening. I was in a daze, and as they continued to hook me up to the fluids, it seemed as if I was watching the events from the outside. My husband finally heard the commotion and awakened in a stupor. "What's the matter? What's the matter?" he asked. The nurses continued to work as my husband watched in disbelief. After the nurses finished hooking me up to the fluids, they just closed the green curtain and left.

I looked over at my husband, and I saw that he had a very concerned look on his face. When I asked him what was wrong, he told me nothing. I asked him why I was hooked up to fluids and he told me that I had gotten sick. I could vaguely remember the nurses scurrying and hovering over me. I felt weak and asked my husband to hand me my Bible from my old brown suitcase. I turned to a scripture in Matthew. I began to read aloud the words on the page from **Matthew 28:19**: *"Go ye therefore and make disciples of all nations, baptizing them in the name of the Father and of the Son and of the Holy Spirit."* When I finished reading, I actually felt as though something happened inside of my body. I was no longer weak. I felt revived. I sat up in the bed as though nothing had ever happened. I looked at my husband and said, *"You know you should have been preaching the gospel a long time ago."* The Lord gave me that scripture for you. In hindsight, I can laugh and say*, isn't that sometimes just like us,* "The word of God is probably for someone else, not for us. **Psalm 19:6-9**

Shortly afterwards, one of the nurses entered the room. She pushed the curtain back and was surprised to see me sitting up in the bed with my Bible in my lap. She went and brought the other nurses into the room. They all looked puzzled and asked me what happened. I told them that I did not know but that I felt much better. The nurse checked all of my vital signs and they were normal. She could not believe it. All of this took place within a matter of minutes. I believe it was "Divine Intervention." Who else but God can turn a tragedy into a triumph in a manner of minutes?

I remained in the hospital an additional day after the physician on call examined me for precautionary measures. The physician did not know what caused the sudden illness. I was told I probably had a strange reaction to the anesthesia. In spite of everything that had previously happened, I felt rejuvenated and better than I had felt in years.

When I was dismissed from the hospital, I was given strict instructions and was confined to bed rest. It was imperative that I wear a hard plastic neck brace for eight weeks. I was not allowed to reach, lift, stoop, or bend. I needed someone with me during my weeks of recovery. A couple of my relatives cared for me during the day and my husband and children at night. They were all wonderful, especially my youngest daughter. When she came home from school, she stayed nestled beside me almost clinging. I felt like something was wrong with her, but I did not know what it could be. When I asked her if something was wrong, she would always answer no. I figured she probably was concerned about my surgery and the separation from her during the hospital stay.

One day, as I went outside to get some sunshine, she came and sat beside me. She told me she needed to talk. She became very serious and said she needed to share something with me. She asked me to promise that I would not tell anyone because they would think she was crazy. I promised. I speak now at her permission. She was twelve years old at the time and this is her story as told to me:

"I was sleeping in my bed the night before you were to come home from the hospital. I was afraid. I thought the doctors had cut part of your neck off, so I was crying. All of a sudden, I saw this bright light shining across the room. I slowly pulled the covers completely from over my eyes and I saw "Big Mama". I am not talking about a ghost or anything, I am talking about a "real person." She was far, far away, yet she seemed close. She asked me, "How old are you now? About 12 years old? "I was too afraid to answer. I started crying. She then said, "Stop crying, your mother is going to be alright. <u>You always were a chicken</u>!" Then, she just left! I looked at the clock and climbed into bed with Val. Val was upset and told

me I had better get back into my own bed and go to sleep. It was 2:00 in the morning. Since I was afraid to move, I stayed in bed with her."

After telling me her story, she looked up at me and asked me if I thought she was crazy. I put my arms around her and told her of course not, I didn't think that. My mind drifted back to that night in my hospital room. It was exactly 2:00 in the morning when I saw my grandmother and cried out to her. The words my daughter spoke were similar to the words I had spoken that night in my hospital room. I can remember crying out in desperation, "Big Mama, I don't want to die. My baby is only 12 years old!" My daughter said she heard my grandmother speak similar words as she stood by her bedside in her room that night. There was no way my daughter knew the words I had spoken in the hospital room. Even now, I do not understand this experience, but I know it was not a dream. But was it a "near death" experience? Is there such a thing? I don't know. But as it is written:

"Eye has not seen, nor ear heard,

Nor have entered into the heart of man

The things which God has prepared for those who love Him."

But God has revealed them to us by His Spirit.

I Corinthians 2:9-10

Maybe one-day God Himself will reveal to me through His Spirit what happened that night, but until then I will just call it a very *"strange phenomenon."*

Who Can Help Me?

It was a blessing to be up and about after my surgery. My recovery went well. After my final checkup, my physician released me to go back to work. Most of the time off was due to my workmen's compensation claim. By this time, I had already been off work almost two years. I had gone to my attorney and told him I would be going back to work. He advised me against it because it would not be good for my case. But the surgery, time off, and other financial issues had been more stressful and emotional than my physical problems. Because of that, I was ready to return to work and back to my normal routine. Therefore, I went to my attorney and asked to have the claim dropped. I dropped my workmen's compensation claim just so that I could return to work. After all, I felt fine. My attorney informed me that my place of employment was not obligated to hire me back; of course, I did not understand why they would have to hire me "back" if I was still an employee.

When I took my physician's statement and attempted to return to work, I discovered that my attorney was correct. When I entered the building and security sought my clearance, it was denied. I was somewhat surprised. What was going on? I was still an employee. I sat in my car praying and not knowing what to do. Finally, I drove off and went home. Since my place of employment was a subsidiary, I called the parent company and informed them of what happened. Within an hour, the president at the local plant called and apologized and told me there was an error and I would be hearing from my supervisor.

The following week, I received a phone call from my immediate supervisor informing me that everything was in place and she would be glad to have me back. When I returned to work, I took my *physician's statement* to my supervisor. The statement had specific instructions for my return. The company was to make sure that my desk and chair had very specific measurements. The letter indicated that I must have an ergonomic work station. Though my supervisor gave the letter to health services, somehow it must have fallen through the cracks. It never happened!

Consequently, I went back to the same work environment that had caused my past illnesses and condition. After the first month, my neck began to hurt and my legs began to get numb. It was obvious that even after surgery, I could no longer do this type of work, especially since no changes had been made to my workstation. After six months of working steadily, my condition worsened. After seeing my health rapidly decline, my husband and I discussed the situation and decided it was not worth it. I would have to quit my job. I didn't know what else to do. I probably could have started the whole legal process over again, but at this point I was emotionally drained and had become weary with fighting the system.

Reluctantly, I resigned from my job. This was a major decision because I would have no income and our family would have no insurance. By this time, our two older boys were in college and we had a mortgage and other expenses. To make matters worse, my husband's painting business was almost bankrupt. Instead of painting their new constructions, most contractors then used a new process called *"stuccoing."* One company had even reneged on one of his painting contracts and chose to use *"Stucco."* He only had two small contracts that would bring income but after that, we would be in yet another financial bind.

I thought I could get unemployment, but for some reason I was denied. As our finances diminished, I knew we needed another miracle. Again, all we could do was pray and trust God. We had no one else to turn to since we had already received help from our caring relatives and friends. We had exhausted all of our resources. But thanks be to God, that after four months of juggling our expenses, our prayers were answered. Again, I received a phone call from my coworker (Vickie) who was also a very good friend. She asked if I requested my stock. I told her no. She reminded me that I had money invested in the company. I had been so distraught over so many things that I had forgotten that for the past ten years, I had paid a small amount each week into company stock. She also informed me the company was changing all of the desks, chairs, and computer tables to sleek ergonomic furniture in every office.

When I left the company, I had written a letter to the corporate office informing them of my experience. I was thankful that something in the letter caught their attention, and they somehow understood the need to make changes. These were much needed changes that would help both the company and its employees. I did not wish the pain of the *"silent killer"*, RSI (Repetitive Stress Injury), upon anyone else. Though it did not help my particular situation at the time, I was grateful that the company made the necessary changes for others. This proved to me that one person can make a difference, and that we can find joy in the midst of our struggles just by helping others. Sometimes, we may not reap the benefit of our labor but others do. Many times, we have to make changes and even suffer for the common good. There are times in life when God uses our sufferings that we may help and save others. ***II Corinthians 1:3-4*** I suppose this is what happened in my situation, and I believe I was all the more blessed for it.

While I was out of work, I decided to enroll in college as a nontraditional student and had one of the best learning experiences ever at a major university in my area. Without knowing it, the kind professors, students, and pleasant environment were restoring my faith in mankind. I majored in Communication/Public Relations. My advisor was a soft-spoken British professor whom I will never forget. Each night of class was most enjoyable and even somewhat therapeutic. Once I entered into the classroom each night, I forgot about my problems.

Within a few weeks, around the time that I had to pay for books and other supplies, I received a check from my previous employment. The letter stated that because of my resignation, my stock investments had to be withdrawn. Since I had dropped my workmen's compensation claim, the company also had to give me a lump sum for my time of disability. These checks gave us some financial relief, but we knew we would have to make some other changes in order to continue to maintain our household. My husband made the decision to close his paint business and began to work as a salesman for a local paint business. This gave us a steady income for a while. However, we still did not have any benefits. It took us about nine months, but by the end of the year, our finances were somewhat stable. We were blessed that we had no more major illnesses during that time, especially since we had no insurance. For the first time in almost three years, we felt financially stable. (Oh, by the way we had become *"true"* tithers.) I say "true", because at first, we were just focused on systematically giving and ten percent, but after a while, we found ourselves giving above and beyond without even knowing it, even in our lack. We had begun also to teach our children and other youth tithing principles, which they say they never forgot. The small children enjoyed getting a dime on the dollar. Today, when I did the same lesson, I tested the children and they were not impressed with one dollar. I had to begin teaching them with 5 dollars then 10. Here again, children are given so much more than our parents gave us. And I must say sadly, that many of them appreciate it, all the less. However, even so, a dollar won't but buy very much these days! Nevertheless, I think we finally got our point across. All the glory for our learning and our teaching belonged to God because we know that without Him, we would not have made it, so we could share our knowledge and wisdom with others.

With hearts of thanksgiving, my husband and I began to praise God and read the Bible even more. We had a sudden leap of faith. I began reading the Bible while I was at home during the day and my husband began reading at night. During our first ten years of marriage, somehow, we had a lapse in our faith. As I stated earlier, somewhere between high school and having children, God was not a priority in our daily lives. Our eldest son was almost ten years old before we returned to any type of corporate worship. Honestly, for the majority of the 70's, we hardly ever attended church. Even when we did attend, we were not serving God wholeheartedly. We only went to church because our parents prompted us. But God has His way of bringing His people back into fellowship with Him. Due to our illnesses and other trials of life, we had rededicated our lives to Christ. I guess it sometimes takes that for *some* of us.

During this time, we began to develop a relationship with God, but it was not until the later years, that we began to fully rely on Him. We had finally learned to depend on the Holy Spirit as our guide. Our illnesses had reminded us: *"That our life was but a vapor that appears for a little time and it could be snuffed away in a moment"* **James 4:14**. We were convinced that our lives were in God's hand, and day by day, our faith was being renewed. It was hard to imagine that it had taken us so long to get to this point.

Oddly enough, it appears that many young married couples and young singles leave the church. I don't think anyone really knows why. There have been many articles written and surveys done, and there are many reasons given for this shift in their church attendance. Some believe that it is boredom, religiosity, and disenchantment. I am of the opinion that no one understands the exact cause of those who leave the church or lose their faith in God. I cannot pinpoint any particular reason I stopped attending church, but somehow, it just happened. Even now I can't believe it took us as long as it did to get back into church and reconnect with God. However, with virtual church and other modern-day conveniences, we see another trend taking place.

But all in all, we went to church and began to trust God during our sicknesses, trials and tribulations. And sometimes we still found ourselves sometimes lost and on the wrong path. But through all of our trying times, we somehow found our way back into the arms of God and still in the arms of each other. I could truly relate to the psalmist who wrote the words: *"Before I was afflicted, I went astray, but now I keep your word"* **Psalm 119:67**. After twenty-two years of marriage with many seasons of sickness, sin, sorrow, sacrifice, and suffering, even now after fifty-two years, we still find ourselves in that same place of thanking God for His word and His goodness.

"For God is not unjust to forget your work and labor of love which you have shown towards His name and that you have ministered to the saints, and do minister. **Hebrews 6:10**

Section Four

THE SPIRITUAL JOURNEY

*"The Spirit of the Lord is upon me, for He has
anointed me to preach the Gospel."*

Luke 4: 18

The Calling

His Calling   Her Calling

The Ordination

His Charge   Her Charge

The Assignment

His Assignment   Her Assignment

*"Go therefore and make disciples of all nations,
baptizing them in the name of the Father and of the
Son and of the Holy Spirit."* **Matthew 28:19**

The Calling

The more we studied God's Word, the more our faith in God increased. We also began to see a shift in our relationship. In the early nineties, our lives had begun to stabilize. During this season, the enemy hit hard, because He knew that God was preparing to fulfil His "Master Plan" for our lives, but because of our love for God and each other, and our faith in God and our strong commitment to Christ, we overcame him and He was defeated. By the mid-nineties, it was a new season of our life and I felt completely secure, and did not have to struggle. I also had a very hopeful expectation that something was about to change in our lives.

My husband and I had become very active in church and were excited about our faith. Yet, I was not ready for what happened next. One morning, the minister gave the invitation to Christian Discipleship. This was the time in the church service when he asked if anyone wanted to accept Jesus Christ as our Savior or rededicate our lives to Christ. I was surprised to see my husband walk hurriedly to the front of the church. When the minister asked him what his desire was, he answered boldly that he had accepted the call to preach. I was shocked. How could he do this without discussing it with me? The minister asked me to come up front and join my husband. As I stood beside my husband, I felt nervous and somewhat perplexed. My youngest daughter came up also. She was the only child at home since all the other children were in college. I was disappointed my husband did not tell me he had plans to go into the ministry. Though I knew he had a special calling on his life, I still would like to have known before he announced it publicly. Nonetheless, I hugged him and pledged my support before we took our seats. At the end of the service, the congregation and pastor showered us with words of wisdom and gave us their blessings.

During certain situations, our ride home seems to take longer. This is how it felt as we rode home from church. We were all very quiet. I could not wait to get home to hear my husband's explanation for not sharing his plans with me. We always shared our plans even in the worst of times. Over the past few years, I felt that we had become even more transparent and forthcoming with each other about our thoughts and plans for our lives. Surely, he must have realized how I felt. Apparently, he did not, because when we arrived home, he never mentioned what happened at church. To him, it was just another quiet Sunday afternoon. I tried several times to bring up the subject but for some reason, the words would never leave my lips. I could never get the courage to confront him about this, which was very different because I had never had that problem before. That night, as we lay in bed, the only words I said to him were similar to the words I had spoken to him when I was in the hospital. I hugged him and told him that he knew that God had called him a long time ago. He answered, "Yes, He has called us. Now go to sleep. We have a lot of work ahead of us." Sometimes, he could say the strangest things and I wondered why he had said that God had called "us."

For the next few months, we found ourselves extremely busy. My husband had a lot of training and meetings to attend for the ministry. This caused a drastic change in our schedule. We could no longer go on our weekend fishing trips that we greatly enjoyed. Since he was in training, he wanted to attend as many meetings as possible. We managed to incorporate some of our vacation and leisure time into his ministry travels. There was also a great deal of studying involved, so he spent many hours studying the Bible and trying to understand the ordinances and discipline of the church.

By the end of the year, he had read the entire Bible and all of the church's suggested literature. He had markings on almost every page. I found myself studying all of his required books so I could assist him in preparing for the examination. I too had also become a very avid reader of the Bible and began interpreting scripture for myself and others. I had become a Sunday School teacher and conducted the "Children's

Moment" during the altar call each Sunday morning. We both began to delve more and more into the scriptures daily. Before I realized it, the time for my husband's examination was almost upon us.

A few months before his time to meet the examining board, I became very nervous. I did not understand why I felt the way I did. I reasoned I was just concerned about his examination. My husband finally noticed and questioned me, but I had no answer. As the day of his examination drew nearer, I became all the more nervous. I had many sleepless nights. One night as I lay awake in bed, I heard the words of an old familiar hymn ringing in my ears: "Sweet hour of prayer, sweet hour of prayer, that calls me from a world of care." I felt something tugging at the strings of my heart. I heard music like the voice of a thousand angels. I sat up in bed hoping to find the source behind the music, but I found nothing. Somehow, I knew that God was calling me with urgency through His tender mercy. A little frightened, I very quietly reached for my Bible on the nightstand. That night, I began reading from midnight into the early morning. I only got a few hours of sleep.

But on Sunday morning when I awakened, I felt more refreshed than ever. I was no longer jittery or nervous. My husband, daughter, and I went to church. As usual, we sat on the third pew. Once the minister gave the "Invitation to Christian Discipleship", I found myself walking towards the front of the church. When he asked me what my desire was, I answered boldly, "I have accepted the call to preach." I stood almost dumbfounded because I had just spoken those words. The minister asked my husband and daughter to join me. This felt like Déjà Vu. I could not believe I had actually accepted the call to preach the gospel. Yes, my husband could but not me. After service, the pastor and congregation offered us their blessings. I felt very uncomfortable as I relived the same events that happened to my husband only a year before.

Our drive home was very quiet. When we arrived home, I began cooking dinner as usual. Everyone was in a very tranquil mood. My husband and I never discussed my calling, yet my mind drifted back to the Sunday he had accepted the call to preach. I remembered the feeling of disappointment I had because he had not discussed his plans with me. Now, here I was, a year later in the same predicament. What was I thinking? Why did I not discuss it with him? Maybe he could have talked me out of it. I felt afraid. My mind raced as all kinds of questions came to my mind. Who was I to preach the gospel? I was just a mother and wife. Besides that, I was a woman and I didn't even know if women were allowed to preach the gospel. What had I done? I spent the rest of the afternoon in a whirlwind. I was thinking of all the things that could have brought me to this point and how or whether I could have avoided it.

I began to recall the many hours of Bible study and how I had conducted youth altar calls and Children's Moments for several years. I had taught Bible study to adults and children. I had visited the sick and those in prisons. I had counseled many. But preaching the gospel was different, and I wasn't sure I was ready. I enjoyed what I was doing. It was my desire to support my husband as he preached the gospel and carried out his ministry. I remember asking, "Lord, are you sure you are calling me?" As I sat there pondering over my calling, I began to feel like a lot of the servants of God whom I had read. Moses said, "I am slow of speech." Jeremiah said, "I am too young." The apostle Paul said, "I have persecuted Christians", and I said, "I am a woman, and besides that I am not prepared for this.

As I retreated into my quiet place that evening, I thought about Mary, Miriam, Deborah, and Huldah. Did they go through this same dilemma? Had God poured His Spirit upon me that I might preach? As I sat quietly and folded my hands, they were as hot as fire. Like the Prophet Jeremiah, I knew there was the fire of the Word of God shut up in my bones. My mind suddenly flashed back to that night in my hospital room. When I read the scripture in **Matthew 28**, was it for me also? Was God commissioning me to go? Without knowing it, had I already accepted the call before that eventful Sunday morning? I had no answers, but I found myself like the Apostle Paul in the Book of Acts when he was on the road to Damascus. All I could say was: "Lord what will thou have me to do?" All I heard was that same little word resounding in my ears: "Go!" So that night I met God in my room. Though the room was dark, suddenly it was as if it was filled with light. I began to worship and praise God as I had never done before. As the tears fell from my eyes, I felt a release and a sigh of relief. I felt the weight of sin, sickness, pain, hurt and even the shadow of death being emptied from inside. As I asked God for forgiveness of my sins and continued to say the words, "I will go", I was filled with indescribable peace and the sudden need to go out and tell the world about the God who saved me, healed me, healed my husband, and raised my children. I wanted to tell the world about the God who helped me and made me whole. Now, I understood why my husband said God had called "us" and we had work to do. I finally understood why he did not discuss his calling with me or I with him. I came to understand that each man, woman, or even child's calling is a matter between him and God. And so, it was with my husband and me. Though my husband and I were a couple, God had called us individually so that we might work out our own salvation as we answered the call to work "faithfully together" in His vineyard. *Philippians 2:12-13*

The Ordination

By the year of 1993, both my husband and I had accepted our calls and found ourselves engaged in constant prayer and study. Since my husband had entered into ministry before me, he was to be ordained in a few months. That year, we had to attend an annual church meeting for those in the ministry. Since I would not be ordained, I would not have to attend all of the various sessions. However, when I arrived at the meeting, I was informed that one of the officers in charge needed to have a brief meeting with me. I was told that it was urgent. Once I found him, he greeted me and offered me a chair. I preferred to stand since it would be brief. He began the conversation by telling me that he knew I wanted to be ordained with my husband. He was correct even though I did not know how he knew. I had prayed a few weeks before the meeting and asked God if it were at all possible that I would like to be ordained with my husband. I had told no one other than God, not even my husband. The officer continued to explain the situation to me. He looked at me and said, "Here's the deal. I have two small churches that need a pastor. I need you to accept the assignment to pastor both churches." I was floored. I had just accepted the call to preach a few months before and now he wanted *me* to pastor not one, but two churches. I had never been a pastor. Surely, there must be some kind of mistake. I was sure there were many other experienced preachers anxiously awaiting the opportunity to pastor even one small church. "Why me?" I asked. The officer told me this was a "Special Assignment" and I would be ordained as such under "Missionary Rule" of the church which meant I was to be ordained under special circumstances. He informed me that if I agreed to accept the assignment to pastor the two small churches, I would be ordained that night alongside my husband. However, if I refused, I could have to wait up to three years before I get ordained. He let me know that he needed an answer immediately. His statement was more of a command than a request. At this point, I began to feel intimidated. I became very irritated. I told him I could not give him an answer right then. I needed to talk to my husband. But most of all I needed to talk to God. He answered very curtly, "Well go and pray, but I need an answer ASAP!" He walked out and closed the door. Stunned, I stood in the middle of the floor. I left the room and went to look for my husband. Thank God, it was almost time for a break so he would be out of the meetings soon. When I found him, I told him about my meeting with the officer. He told me to find a quiet place to pray. Unlike me, he was always so calm and level-headed. I took his advice and found a quiet spot where I could pray and sort out my thoughts. I found myself stopping at the nearest shopping mall but not to shop. I went into the ladies' powder room and prayed a very simple prayer. I told the Lord that I didn't know what to do. Before I could even finish, I heard the same small word that rang in my ears when I accepted the call to preach. "Go." I went and found the officer and told him that I would go. His whole attitude seemed to change. I couldn't understand why his attitude changed and he seemed so relieved. He seemed overly excited, and told me I had made the right decision. He shook my hand before he left the room. He told me he was adding my name to the list of candidates for ordination. It was settled. I would be ordained that night alongside my husband. I found my husband and gave him the exciting news. We didn't fully understand any of it, but we were sure that it was all in God's plan.

Later that afternoon, we both had an examination on the Bible and various other disciplines of the church. I was familiar with most of the information because I had studied with my husband even before I accepted the call. Isn't it interesting how God prepares us for tasks even before we know we are assigned? We both passed the examination with flying colors and we were told we would be ordained that night at seven o'clock. We left the meeting full of excitement and anxious for the ordination service to take place.

When we returned to the church that night, we were advised to sit on the front pew with several other men and women who were to be ordained. Though I was excited, I still couldn't believe all of this was happening so quickly. When they called the names of the candidates for ordination, they called my name immediately after my husband's. As we stood around the altar, my mind flashed back to when we were in the seventh grade at the fine arts festival. During the fine arts festival, though we were on the same team, we performed on stage separately. I thought about the day we stood before the judge to be married. I thought about the day I accepted my call. But this time was different. As we stood together at the altar, we were united as one, but I felt another presence. I knew it was the presence of the Lord. I began to see the plan of God unfold before my eyes. I knew we were standing on "Holy Ground." As we then kneeled at the altar, I closed my eyes to pray and I felt a flood of tears trickling down my face. I suddenly realized how God had called two people together at an early age to enjoy our childhood lives together and learn from one another. Through our years of growing up, we experienced the many joys and pleasures of life and even shared in each other's pain, before He ushered us into adulthood.

That night, I began to understand the words of the psalmist: *"He possessed our reins and knew us in our mother's womb"* **Psalm 139:13**. He knew the thoughts and plans he had for us, long before we did **Jeremiah 29:11.** For God had created my husband and me as male and female to one day be joined into holy matrimony. At the appointed time, He had joined us together to become one spirit in Him. He was using us even as children, and we didn't even know it. It is amazing how God uses all kinds of situations and all types of people to fulfill His purpose. For as unusual and unorthodox as this situation was, my husband and I were ordained that special night. Normally, we would stand together but on the night of our ordination, we knelt side by side in the presence of God. God was humbling us so that we could be used by Him.

He had already set the day and time of our ordination. It was not about me, my husband, or even the leader who summoned me to his office, but God himself had called us to be ordained that very moment. Unknowingly, we had been set aside years before He actually called us. I was humbled to know that even before we knew God and were ready to preach His Word, God had looked beyond our faults and our failures and made us His own. *"For we are His workmanship, created in Christ Jesus for good works which God prepared beforehand that we should walk in them"* **Ephesians 2:10.** Our ordination was not the beginning, but a continuation of the walk down a path that started long ago.

The closing of the ordination service was very moving. I felt chills as the spiritual leader placed his right hand on my head. I savored every word of the charge he gave us. When we returned home that night, my husband and I were still in a very quiet mood. We didn't have very much to talk about. I think we were still considering the events of the day and what effect they would have on our lives. We did not ponder for long since we still had a few more days of workshops and meetings to attend. Having more questions than answers, we agreed to set everything aside and go to bed.

The Assignments

We attended several more days of meetings and worship services. Finally, on a Friday afternoon, church appointments were given. Many of the pastors waited anxiously to hear their appointments to their assigned churches. The overseer and the leader were responsible for assigning pastors to all of the churches in their particular districts. I didn't know the names or locations of the churches I would be assigned. I just knew I would be sent out to pastor two churches. As I sat waiting to hear the names of the appointees, just thinking about having to lead a group of people caused me great fear. I did not even know how or where to start. Just the thought of having the responsibility of leading two churches when I had just accepted the call was even more frightening. I also had fears of my husband being assigned to a different church and our family not being able to worship together on Sunday.

During my husband's travels selling paints, he had passed a small church that appeared to be closed. He had inquired about this church and found that this church was under the jurisdiction of an overseer. The overseer was the spiritual leader over the officer and all of the churches in a designated region. My husband located the overseer's phone number and called him. When he called, the overseer informed him that the little church had been closed for several years because it had very few members. He told him he would like to have a pastor to accept the challenge of re-opening the church. My husband told him he would be interested in re-opening the church. This conversation occurred approximately three months before the annual meeting. He never heard any more from the overseer so he did not know the final outcome. But sure enough, on the last day of the meeting, when the appointments were read, my husband received the assignment to reopen the church. This was his first assignment, and it was fifty-five miles from our home. I waited anxiously for my assignments, and it seemed as though my name would never be called. Finally, as the last few appointments were read, I was assigned two small churches in our hometown: I had two church assignments. Sadly, my fears of being in separate locations were confirmed.

At the end of the meeting, one of the pastors came up to congratulate us. He told us that he would be praying for us. Then, he began to tell my husband about the church to which he had been assigned. The pastor informed him there were only two members in the church. One member was an eighty-four-year-old woman who lived in the town, and the other was a young lady who lived sixty miles away from the church. This had been her grandparent's church so she remained faithful and attended whenever she had the opportunity. He also informed my husband that he had served as pastor of the church a few years before it was closed, and it had been very challenging. My husband thanked him for the information.

Although I waited, no one came to offer any information about my two churches. After speaking with the pastor, we were anxious to get home. We were both exhausted. This was the first time we had attended the annual meetings in several days. Due to our work schedule, we usually attended twice a week, but that particular week, we had to attend most sessions. We were glad when the meetings were over so that we could visit the churches to which we had been assigned. Although my husband was familiar with his church, he had only looked inside of it through a window. My story was far different. As far as I knew, I had never seen the churches that were assigned to me. The spiritual overseer had given my husband a key and contact information for his members. I did not have keys to either of my assigned churches; however, I was much too tired to worry about that then. I only wanted to go home and rest.

When we arrived home, I wanted to forget about our meetings and my new assignments. But once inside, I was greeted by the steady beeping sound of our answering machine, indicating there were several messages. As I hit the button and began to retrieve them, I found that all of the messages were from members of one of my assigned churches. One member was calling to get permission to have a wedding rehearsal and needed a key. Another message stated that I needed to go visit a family who had a death. There were several other messages about members who were sick. And still another message from a member who wanted to know if he could use the church for a funeral, but he made sure to tell me another pastor would officiate and preach the eulogy. My own uncertainty made me believe it was probably due to the fact that I was a woman and a novice. I had planned to give the members my contact information on the first Sunday, but I guess they already had it. I was overwhelmed and had not started my ministry. Or so I thought. I guess I had.

Before I responded to any of my messages, I began questioning how I would handle all of these situations that had been so abruptly placed upon me. I prayed. I told God, I had never been a pastor before, *as if He didn't know!* I guess I was one now whether I knew what to do or not. I still could not figure out how or why I had been given the responsibility of two churches when I had yet to learn how to pastor one church. It just didn't make sense to me. Once again, having more questions than answers, my husband and I agreed to set everything aside and go to bed.

We had planned to sleep late since we had been in meetings all week; however, we were awakened early the next morning by the doorbell. My husband dressed as quickly as possible and opened the door. A few minutes later, he came into the room and handed me several keys. He told me our visitor was a church officer from one of the churches. He had come to drop off the keys and to give me directions to the church. He told my husband they had services on first and third Sundays. He also told him they had about fifty members.

Around noon, one of the officers from the church of my second assignment, also came with a set of keys and briefed me about the church. He informed me that they had only fifteen members and they held church service on fourth Sunday. I found all of this to be unbelievable and quite distressing. I wondered what the members did on the other Sundays of the month. This meant that between the two churches I would only have services three Sundays out of each month. This would be a major adjustment for me because I attended church every Sunday.

When we drove up to the first church, I was in amazement. The church was in need of major repairs. The roof, porch and siding, all needed much work. The yards also needed some care, especially the cemetery, nearby.

When we entered the inside of the church, someone was in the process of removing old carpet, but had not finished the job. The bathroom facilities were inoperable and there was an unfinished addition in the back. I could see that the leader who sent me there knew there was much work to be done. When I walked through the church I had tears in my eyes, because I could see that the people needed some direction and their spirits needed to be uplifted. They had been neglected for so long by their organization that they had lost hope. As I left the church, I was determined with Holy Spirit, them and me, we could make things better. As I walked outside, I asked God, the same question, that was asked in Ezekiel in the thirty-seventh chapter, "Can these bones live? Upon leaving, I knew that I would do everything, I could to revive them again, and I would with God's help. *Zechariah 4:6*

In time, I went back into the sanctuary with my husband close behind me. I knelt down at the old wooden altar and wept. I don't know if I was weeping for the church or for myself. While I was sobbing, I can remember my husband's hand on my shoulder. Looking back, over the years, he was always a solemn comforter, strong supporter, and faithful friend to me, as well as others. I remember, he kept telling me, that everything would be alright, and I would be fine. Those were the same last words of love, support and comfort, that he gave before he closed His eyes the week before he took His eternal rest from labor to reward.

After kneeling at the altar that day, I finally stood to my feet, gathered my composure, and walked out the back door. My husband locked all of the doors, and we drove off to the next church. After my first experience, I had no idea of what to expect from the next church. We drove only a few miles to my other church assignment. When we arrived, I realized I was familiar with this church. When

I was a little girl, I had passed by this church many times with my father. He had lots of drinking buddies in this area. From the outside, this church looked much better than the last one. The grass had been freshly cut which was already a good sign. When we went inside, there was a very small sanctuary that was, to my surprise, very nice. Just as I was about to celebrate the victory of having at least one church that did not have to be overly attended to, I was shocked to discover that the church did not have a restroom. I could not believe that there was a church in the 90's without a restroom. Though the toilet was almost inoperable at the other church, at least it had one that could be fixed. This church did not have one at all. We didn't stay at the second church very long. My husband locked the door, and now it was time to visit his church.

When we arrived at his assigned church, I found a very pleasant surprise. There stood a small, quaint red brick building with a well-manicured lawn. Not only was it well kept on the outside, but it was immaculate on the inside. As soon as we walked into the church, there were separate bathrooms in the front of the church. Not only that, but there was a pastor's study with a small restroom inside as well. In the rear of the church, there was a kitchen and fellowship hall. I was amazed at the contrast. Only God knew what His purpose was in all of this because even though the spiritual overseer had called out the appointments, God had made the assignments. He had assigned my husband to a small immaculate church with only two members, and assigned me to two small churches with more members but whose buildings needed a lot of care. I was at a loss at this point. Again, I just fell down at the altar and wept. Once I got up, my husband locked the church and we started home.

After we left, my husband wanted to visit his eighty-four-year-old church member who lived only a few blocks from the church. He had already received her contact information from the overseer at the meeting. When we visited her, she welcomed us into her home. I was surprised because she looked much younger than her actual age. Her hair was in a beautiful bun. She was well-dressed and exuded a lot of energy. Before we left, she handed my husband a very old checkbook. She informed him that the account was very low and there was no money to give him a salary. My husband didn't seem concerned about her statement. She told him they had about three hundred dollars in the account. After thanking her for her kindness, we said our goodbyes and started back home. From the car, I looked back to take a quick glimpse at the little red brick church on the side of the road, and I began to laugh. I looked over at my husband and said, "God really does have a sense of humor. He has assigned you to a church without people and me to a people without a church." Though our callings and assignments were separate, somehow, they were inextricably intertwined.

During the rest of the ride home, I was engrossed in a private conversation with the Lord. I needed an explanation and help. Since I did not receive any answers to my questions, I would just have to wait and see. How would a husband-and-wife team of new pastors handle three churches in different towns and on different Sundays? I was trying to figure out the schedule in my mind before I could put it on paper. The annual meeting ended the last Saturday in July and the fourth Sunday was approaching. I would see one congregation that Sunday. My husband would also have to drive 55 miles to his for his first service. Our youngest daughter had asked to attend worship at our home church on fourth Sundays. We agreed because we thought it would be good for her to still spend some time in worship with her friends. This was going to be very different for us as a family.

I would not see the other congregation for another week since they only had service on the *first* and *third* Sundays. The next Sunday we would all attend church there. Since neither of my churches had service on the *second* and *fifth* Sundays, we would all go back with my husband on those Sundays. What appeared to be a major problem was not a problem at all. We would only be separated on *fourth* Sunday. It is amazing how we are trying to figure out solutions to problems that God has already answered. In this situation, God was revealing His many truths to us. The truths that we had read so intently in our Bibles were constantly being brought to life. I saw the Word in **Romans 8:28** and this great truth came to life in this situation: *"And we know that all things work together for good to those who love God, to those who are the called according to His purpose."*

First Sunday Morning

The following morning, we all got up and headed for our destinations not knowing exactly what to expect. We left our home early so that I would have time to take our youngest daughter to church and get to my own church early as well. My husband had to leave home an hour earlier than us as his drive was much further. I hated that he had to go alone, but so did I.

It took only a few minutes for me to arrive for worship at my church. When I arrived, the officer was waiting for me at the church entrance. Once I entered the sanctuary, all of the members greeted me with a very warm welcome. Most of the members were elderly, but there were several young women with children. Before I went into the pulpit, I took special care to ask the children their names. They were full of energy and excitement. I couldn't wait to find out more about them, after service.

When it was time for service to begin, I was a little nervous about standing before the people. Of course, I had stood before many audiences at fine arts festivals and competitions but preaching before a congregation was different. With God's help, I finished my message entitled *"I am the Resurrection and the Life" from the book of John.* Even before I was called to preach, over the years, I found myself scribbling messages and titles in the margins of certain scriptures, and this was one of those.

From the pulpit, I had noticed a man in a royal blue suit, sitting alone on the back row. I think I had seen him walking that way before with a guitar. As I opened my Bible, he appeared to listen very attentively. Once I finished my message, I gave the invitation for anyone who would like to accept Jesus Christ in their life. I saw him wipe his eyes and then he headed toward the front. He said He needed Jesus in his life. I didn't know if he was rededicating himself, so I just read and discussed *John 3:16* and *Romans 10:9-13*. I later learned that he died within the next few days. I was thankful that God had me to give a word about His love, forgiveness, death and resurrection. I was told later, that he had gone home and shared his church experience with his family.

Once service was over, I spent some time with the children and the church officer. The officer showed me around and informed me of the work they planned to do in the coming year. Several of the ladies had cooked their special dishes for me. One had even baked a pound cake and I could smell the aroma throughout the service. There was no kitchen so she had it next to her on the front seat. After service, I thanked all of the members and headed home to see how my husband had enjoyed his day.

A Very Blessed Day

I arrived home an hour before he did. By the time he came home, dinner was ready. My daughter had asked to spend the evening with a friend, so she was not at home. When he arrived, he took off his robe and immediately began to tell me about his day. He told me when he arrived at the church, he was surprised to find that several hymnals were placed on the pulpit and on the pews. The bathroom cabinets had been filled with supplies. These items were not there when we visited the day before. When he went to the pastor's study, there was a thermos filled with water. The eighty-four-year-old member who lived nearby had brought the supplies. She informed him when we visited that due to her illness, she would not be at service fourth Sunday, but he was very pleased she had been so kind, even in her absence. He'd been sure to call her before service to thank her for her hospitality.

That Sunday he had ten people to attend service. The young lady who was an out-of-town member came and brought some of her family members with her. He also had several other people from the community to come and join during the service. He felt that many of them probably came out of curiosity upon hearing the church had been reopened. Whatever the reason, he was grateful to have them. He told me that many had promised to return, especially since some of them did not have church service on fourth Sunday at their own church. All in all, he too had a very fulfilling and blessed day.

After hearing about his day, I told him I had a surprisingly pleasant day as well. We relaxed for a while and then sat down to eat. Just seeing the pound cake reminded me of the pound cakes my grandmother baked filled with sugar and the taste of vanilla. This brought back beautiful memories of the times she would let me help to prepare the batter and I would lick the spoon. I spent a lot of time with my grandmother, and I missed her a lot. It was hard to believe she died over seven years ago (1986). I went to church with her quite often, and I wondered what she would think of me becoming a pastor. Her church would never think of ordaining a woman. I laughed at the thought of my grandmother and then my thoughts went to my mother who was quite stable at this time. The physician's had prescribed her medication that seemed to help her a lot more. She even had a few sessions with a therapist every month. However, I believe it came somewhat too late. Most of her issues were deeply embedded, and she still felt strongly that she had been cheated out of a life of happiness. At least at this point in her life, she was able to stay alone. She was seventy-five years old at this time.

When she found out I had been called to preach, she told me she was very proud of me and she *guessed now*, she would have to begin believing in "women preachers." *Oh! But for the love of mothers!* Of course, many of my relatives did not approve of it either, but I understood. I had a lot of challenging work before me, and I couldn't spend time worrying about what others thought. I held fast to the words of the song, "A charge to keep I have and a God to glorify." These words gave me the strength to make preparation and embark upon the ministry before me.

I had to schedule board meetings and church planning meetings for both churches; consequently, I had to spend a lot of time consulting God and seeking His direction. My husband and I were in unfamiliar territory, but we had learned to put our trust in God, *"For we walk by faith, not by sight."* **II Corinthians 5:7** In spite of our inexperience, it was our heart's desire to please God as we blessed and showed love to His people.

My Other Assignment

Immediately after preaching at my fourth Sunday charge, I began preparing my sermon for the first Sunday at my other assignment. I only had one week of preparation. However, God had already given a word for the people. Though I was somewhat nervous, I was excited about meeting them and proclaiming God's Word. I was even more nervous about standing before the people at this church than I was at the other one. This very intense sense of nervousness was probably because I had already heard rumors that the members of this church definitely did not want a "female" as pastor.

I arrived at church extra early, so I could spend some time in prayer. Since my husband did not have a church that Sunday, he came with me, and our daughter came as well. I was grateful because we could all take Holy Communion together and I was happy that they were there to support me. As I walked into the church, I was moved with compassion when I went inside and noticed that someone had placed new carpet on the floor and moved the old piano. My feelings soon changed into excitement. I became eager to meet the congregation and wondered if I knew any of the members of the church.

By the time church service was to begin, I had no idea who or if anyone would actually show up. Though they trickled in slowly, by eleven o'clock, there were about fifty people seated in the congregation. That morning, when I looked over the new congregation, I saw only one familiar face. I had seen her at several programs at a friend's church, but all of the other people were strangers to me.

I started the service on time. My husband prayed and the congregation sang a few songs. Though my husband sat in the pulpit with me, I knew this was a task I had to do on my own. After the people brought their offerings, it was almost time for the sermon. As

I looked throughout the congregation, it seemed as if all eyes were fixed upon me. As I looked into their faces, I remembered a scripture I had read in the book of **Ezekiel in chapter two** when Ezekiel had to speak to a group of people. God told Ezekiel not to be afraid of the people's faces or their looks. After the choir sang another hymn, I said a silent prayer, stood up boldly, and faced the congregation. I glanced over to my left at a group of women seated together. One of the ladies in an oversized white hat with a long blue feather on its side flashed me an assuring smile. This gave me the strength to go forward. Once again, it was one little smile that made all the difference in the world. This elderly woman, whom they called the "Mother" of the Church, became my most devoted friend and a cherished servant to our church all the days of her life. After I returned her smile, I opened my mouth and began to preach from *Isaiah 61:1-2*:

"The Spirit of the Lord God is upon me and he has anointed me to preach good tidings unto the meek; he hath sent me to bind up the brokenhearted, to proclaim liberty to the captives, and the opening of the prison to them that are bound, to proclaim the acceptable year of the Lord and the day of vengeance of our God; to comfort all that mourn...KJV

After speaking those few words, I knew that God had indeed called me to preach His gospel to His people. Once I finished my message, I felt as if I had emptied everything that was within me. Even now, that same feeling is with me whenever I preach God's Word.

Once I spoke blessings upon the people through the benediction, the service was ended. I stood at the front entrance and shook hands with all of the members and friends who had come.

They thanked me for the message and offered me their support. I met all of the officers of the church and laughed with a few of the children. I also met the youth director and youth choir president. I could not wait to become involved with the youth ministry at the church since this had always been my passion. After a very eventful day, my husband and I prepared to make the drive to our home.

At the end of the day, I knew we had reached yet another milestone in our marriage in that we had been able to support one another in our God-given assignments. Once again, "We were a team." In spite of my many reservations, with God's help through His Spirit, my day had gone quite well. I had already begun to meditate on a message for the third Sunday. My text would be taken from **Ezekiel chapter thirty-seven**. I felt the urge to ask the congregation, "Can These Bones Live?" This was a question I had asked God when I first visited the church. I couldn't believe it, but I was already excited and couldn't wait to stand before the people again.

After about six months, it seemed as if we were settled in our ministry and in tune with our congregations. The congregations began to grow, and my husband was sent to minister to people in his community more so than the members of his congregation. The young man whom he mentored realized his calling and became a minister of the gospel. Through the guidance of the Holy Spirit, we became very useful and profitable servants that year. We enjoyed our ministry and knew that God was still leading us on our journey.

Interestingly enough, almost a year after I had gained my confidence, I received some disturbing news. I had attended one of our out-of-town church meetings and a young lady came up to speak to me. She asked me how I was managing as a new "female" pastor with two churches. I told her it was not as taxing as I thought it would be. She gave me a coy look and made a cynical remark. She told me that she bet some of the leading district officers were already trying to "get rid" of me. When I didn't understand, she looked at me and asked, "You really don't know?" The look on my face must have given her the answer because she invited me to sit down on a nearby bench. She said she had an inside track of the annual church assignments. She informed me that the reason I had been assigned two churches was because I was somewhat outspoken and a woman. There had been hopes that I would upset some of the officers, and this would disperse the members into several larger churches in the area. This would then lead to several church mergers which were very much needed. This could explain why I was chosen to pastor two churches so early in my ministry, but it was only hearsay. Besides, I knew that God was the one who had ultimately given me the assignments, not the overseer or the officer. Regardless of their motives, I knew God meant it for good, and thankfully, I had enjoyed my first year of ministry. The members of both churches treated me with kindness and respect, so I refused to allow her words to dampen my spirit.

I didn't even attempt to approach the officer or address the issue. It had been almost a year and both churches were doing well and so was my ministry. And even if this rumor turned out to be true, it was a plan that didn't work, and I had too much work to do and too much to learn to waste time on a plan that didn't work. *Acts 5:38* I was not defeated and I give all thanks to God who gives us the victory through our Lord and Savior Jesus Christ". *I Corinthians 15:57.*

Therefore, with my husband beside me, I continued to stand firm in my commitment to serve, for I found that in every situation I encountered the Holy Spirit was equipping my husband and me to become faithful workers in His vineyard and it was my prayer that we both would one day stand together at the "same" church and proclaim the Word of God that His people might be blessed. And that we did, every Sunday, even until the last few weeks of his death.

Section Five

Here We Stand

Two are better than one,

Because they have a good reward for their labor.

For if they fall, one will lift up his companion.

Ecclesiastes 4:9-10

Here We Stand and He Still Gives Me Butterflies

Yes, in late 1994, God called my husband and me into a new ministry as one, and now he is calling us to the close of this assignment, some 30 years, later. When we started our second year of ministry, we asked the overseer if he would give us an assignment together. He gave us the church that I pastored which had the most members. Though this was a new concept for him, he agreed and I will be forever grateful. Unknowingly, we were not to continue serving under him. The very next year, God removed us from that ministry, separated us and set us aside. I am reminded of the Holy Spirit speaking in **Acts 13:2** when He said, "Now separate to Me, Barnabas and Saul for the work to which I have called them." During those times of separation, we did not fully understand God's purpose or His plan, but we had to accept the fact that we were not leaving the place where we were planted but rather God was continuing our ministry in a new field. Starting a new ministry was not easy. We found ourselves standing together preaching the gospel in the dining room of our home. We finally moved into a classroom and then into the school cafeteria. Eventually, we relocated to a local community center, and within a year, we purchased and paid for five acres of land.

The next year, we broke ground for a new church. At this point in our ministry, we found ourselves standing in the presence of God in a world of choices, challenges, and opportunities. We experienced rejection, hardships, and persecution along the way with numerous attacks from the enemy both inside and out. Sometimes our faith waivered but God always stepped in to offer us hope, and at the end of each day, He brought us closer to Him and to each other. We also made many mistakes along the way, from which our faith was increased and we became much stronger.

As we continued on our spiritual journey, we came to realize that God had not brought us together as a couple for ourselves but that He might use us in His work. However, this was no new phenomenon for God had ordained and called couples together well over four thousand years to carry out his plan.

Even more so, it really all started from the beginning in the "Garden of Eden" when God created Adam from the dust, breathed life into him, and then made Eve bone of his bone and flesh of his flesh. After which, he placed them in the garden to work together as husband and wife. There was also Abraham and Sarah, Isaac and Rebekah, Jacob and Leah), and in the New Testament Zachariah and Elisabeth, Mary and Joseph and the most noted couple, Aquilla and Priscilla, but above all Mary and Joseph. All of these couples played a significant role in carrying out God's very intricate and unique plan for couples. God had a specific plan for these couple's lives just as He does for us today.

While on their journey, these great couples had to weather the storms of life as they carried out God's plan. Nevertheless, they continued in faith and so will we. As husbands and wives, we must face challenges, but through it all, we have to learn to trust in God, for He has not left us comfortless. He leads us and guides us through His Spirit. He also left us His Word so that we may gain insight by reading the testimonies and experiences of the lives of couples from ages past.

Through the eyes of Abraham and Sarah, we learned that many times we may have to move to a strange land in order to serve Him. *Genesis 11:31* So, it was with us when we had to leave our familiar church home. Though we were settled in a comfortable place serving God, He chose to move us and we chose to obey Him. When we read of the struggles of Jacob with his first wife Leah, we find that even when we don't understand His plans, God can bless us in every situation and they have purpose. Jesus came from the line of Judah, Jacob and Leah's fourth Son. *Genesis 29:35*

I remember Mary and Joseph, who gave birth in a most unusual manner, in the least likely place at God's appointed time just as we gave birth to a new ministry in a somewhat strange and untraditional way. But theirs is the greatest birth ever. *Luke 2:1-20* This couple was chosen by God to bring to the whole world a Savior and a Deliverer. For God loved the world so much that He gave His only begotten Son that whosoever believes in Him should not perish but have everlasting life *John 3:16*. So, Mary and Joseph brought forth a Son whose name was "Jesus." Mary humbly accepted her call as a wife and a mother and Joseph solemnly accepted his duty as a husband and father. And because of their faith and obedience, *"For unto us, a Child is born, unto us, a Son is given and the government will be upon His shoulder. And His name will be called Wonderful, Counselor, Mighty God, Everlasting Father, Prince of Peace Isaiah 9:6 KJV*

We learn further that sometimes God takes us through many twists and turns in order to get us to His appointed place. I am reminded of our ordination and appointments as unorthodox as they were; God took us to the place which He had reserved for us and He continues to bless us and use us in His work. We remained there standing steadfast in our faith for thirty-three (33) years, until my husband then (bishop) took his eternal rest from his labor on *September 14, 2023*, and my end of assignment notice from God, on *October 14, 2023*.

God is still calling couples today to be fruitful and multiply. He is calling husbands and wives to build Christian families that share His love by preaching and teaching throughout the world. Therefore, it is our mission to share our love of God and our love for each other with our families and the world as they walk with us through our life experiences which have brought us to where we are today. We can relate to the New Testament couple, Aquila and Priscilla who worked together faithfully as they carried the gospel to many people throughout the land as living testimonies for Jesus Christ. *Acts 18:1-4 (Did you ever notice that the order of Aquilla and Priscilla names are sometimes interchanged?)* Interesting! Very Interesting!

God's plan is eternal, and He will continue to ordain and call couples even unto the end of time. He is calling couples in the 21st century to teach, preach, and work in the "field of life" as they lead others to Jesus Christ. He called my husband and me in this century at this appointed time and "Here We Stand", no longer just servants but over time, we became true friends to God and each other *John 15:15.*

We heard His call and we answered it and now I invite you and yours to come into this same "Garden of God's Love" to work together as one in His vineyard. It is refreshing to know that just as we had a misguided and unfaithful beginning, God still loved us and showed us a more excellent way toward the fulfillment of life. We made a solemn promise to God that we would stay together and work for Him until death. And we forever held fast to that promise, until my husband 's death. But even more so, God made a promise to us that if we stand firm and hold steadfast to our faith, He would be with us, and He did. And He is making that same promise to me today, as I travel alone, Holy Spirit with me. He is also making that same promise to you and yours. *Are you ready to accept the charge?*

As I look back over the years, God's love has always been there and we always had an unconditional love for each other. And even after all these years, as my husband closed his eyes, it seemed as though we just met yesterday. And when I sat at his bedside, hurting, but smiling upon his face, he still gave me butterflies! *Maybe that is why I love butterflies!*

Among all of this love and beauty, we did not forget the enemy, who came many times, to kill, steal and destroy us and our marriage, but he was already a defeated foe and could never destroy or separate us from God or each other, even at death. *O death, where is your sting? O' Hades, where is your victory? The sting of death is sin, and the strength of sin is the law. But thanks be to God, who gives us the victory through our Lord Jesus Christ. **I Corinthians 15:55-57***

Solomon in all his wisdom wrote: "Two are better than one because they have a good reward for their labor" ***Ecclesiastes 4:9.*** We have indeed had a good reward for our labor. After sixty-two years of sharing our lives together and over Fifty–two years of marriage, my husband has retired from this life of labor to reward, but he was able to share in the blessings of our sharing together in ministry for over thirty years and seeing our family increase from six to twenty-five with the new addition of two granddaughters-in law, and two great grandchildren. *For this we thank God, and were truly blessed are indeed forever grateful.*

Before we began our journey, we had no idea where the narrow path that connected our two streets and joined us together would take us, but we vowed to travel on it, until death, and we did. But we know it has only been *"divinely severed"* for a season., for we which are alive and remain shall be caught up together with them in, the clouds to meet the Lord in the air, and so shall we ever be with the Lord. *I Thessalonians 4:17* I look forward to that day!

Therefore, be steadfast, immovable, always abounding in the work of the Lord, knowing that your labor is not in vain in the Lord. *I Corinthians 15:58*

May God Bless you and keep you as you carry out His plan for your lives as you advance the kingdom of God.

O God, you have taught me from my youth;

And to this day I declare your wondrous works,

Now when I am old and gray headed,

O God do not forsake me, until I declare

your strength to this generation.

Your power to everyone who is to come.

Also, your righteousness, O God is very high,

You who have done great things; O God, who is like You?

Psalm 71:17-19

Behold New Things Shall Come

My mother and husband who showed their love for me.
My father who planted my "special tree"
My aunt and uncle who took me in
The sudden loss of my dearest friend.

My grandmother's voice that sounded so sweet
All of my friends I loved to greet
My friend who became my mate for life
Disappointments, pains, sorrows and strife
I know they are not here to stay
For all of these things shall pass away.

I hold them as keepsakes in my heart with love
I count them as blessings from God above
I continue in hope and keep the faith
I remember the old things that passed away
I look each day for a bright new morn
Until my work down here is done
Behold! Behold! New things shall come.

Retha Evans Ezell

To Our Mother
(Mae Dear)

This was my first EPILOGUE of *Love Leaps Forward, Time Tilts Backward (2014) which was referred to in revised version of,* "My Forward." (2023)

I close this book and with open eyes I look up to heaven to thank God for my mother:

(Rosa Lee Napier Evans)

In spite of all of her illnesses and tragedies in life, with God's help, my mother beat all odds and raised six wonderful children. She was blessed to see her many children, grandchildren, and even great-great grandchildren.

"Her children rise up and call her blessed."

Proverbs 31:28

In the same month that I closed my "last chapter of my book," she closed the "last chapter of her life" when she entered into her eternal rest on December 11, 2012. I am confident that she was led victoriously into a new life. At death her face had a certain *"heavenly glow"* which we had not seen before. For the first time, there were no more struggles. There was a peace on her face that passed all of our understanding. The peace which she could not achieve in life, somewhere through her faith in Christ, she had achieved at death. And for this, we are all forever grateful.

There are depths of love, that we cannot know, 'til we cross that narrow sea. There are heights of joy that we cannot reach til we rest in peace with Thee. *(Hymn, Draw Me Nearer)*

Children: Catherine Evans Slappey (Douglas),Hudman Evans, Sr., Retha Evans Ezell, (James Calvin), and Patricia Evans

Departed: Winfred Evans, Sr., Alfonzo Evans, Sr., Alvin Evans, Calvin Evans

EPILOGUE

(Time Flies! Love Leaps!)

I can hardly believe that it has been almost a decade, since we published our first book (Love Leaps Forward; Time Tilts Backward.) But it has! Since then, we have seen many changes, and have continued to face many challenges, over the past 10 years, but God is faithful, and "We still have joy in the Holy Ghost, because we have Jesus!" *James 1:2-4, Romans 14:17*

About four years ago, I noticed some changes in my husband's memory. We went for his regular visit. His physician did a cursory memory test, then ordered bloodwork, X-Rays, CT scans and a battery of other tests. After reviewing the results, he referred my husband to a neurologist. After the initial visit and follow-up, the neurologist diagnosed him of having "Frontal Temporal and Vascular Dementia." He informed us, that there was no cure.

However, he did prescribe several medications, which he said could either slow down the condition, speed it up, or no change. He also suggested a "Mediterranean Diet." After which, my husband and I prayed, researched, talked, and finally decided that he would not take any medication. Though, this is not a suggestion for all, but according to our faith, it did work for us. We simply changed his diet (somewhat), kept him active, and prayed that God would, "keep his mind in perfect peace", because we trusted in Him, according to His word in *Isaiah 26:3.* We were at peace with the decision we made. Hallelujah!

But, would you believe, almost two years later, he was diagnosed with cancer? From 1986 until now, this was his fourth cancer diagnosis, yet he lived a full and active life. In 1986, *Fibro- Sarcoma,*

<u>2009</u> bla*dder,* <u>2019</u> *thyroid* and then <u>2023</u> *prostate.* A sudden rise in his PSA level led his physician, to suspect prostate cancer. Once all the testing, and a biopsy was performed, they found that it was indeed prostate cancer and it had already metastasized in his left hip.

Once again, we had to make some hard choices, of whether he would take treatment, medications, or do nothing. We chose no medication or treatment in his early and middle stages. But most of all, I already knew my husband's wishes from past experiences, and he always wanted to enjoy his usual quality of life, as much as possible, until the end. And he did, with the help of <u>Georgia Hospice Care</u>, who respected our wishes as much as feasibly possible, even unto the last hour. It is always important to remember that one's method of medical treatment is a personal matter, and should be of their own choosing.

I was grateful and blessed for even with my husband's illnesses, he still was always a joy to be around for family, friends, church members, and even to strangers that he met at the grocery store, the doctor's office or the parking lot. As he awakened each morning, he seemed to have no worries, he was always calm, at times his mind was sharp, and he came up with many words of wisdom. He was never aggressive or combative, but always jovial, in a good mood, and full of spirit, which was highly unusual, considering his illnesses. Many days, the children and I knew he was in pain, yet he would only accept low dose pain meds, and he never complained. We knew it could only be the grace of God and His blessings.

Speaking of blessings, on January 11, 2023, we had water damage in our home. It was a strange water valve leak that came in like a flood. What seemed like a minor problem, caused water to cover over half of our home? Overall, were displaced for five months. But guess what? Over the months of our going out and coming in, I saw many blessings surface in the midst of the flood, and I am convinced that God was in control of it all.

We stayed, in a very small hotel room where we had very little space and practically no responsibility. Our insurance company and an agent who took very good care of us. My husband and I were able to spend many intimate hours, sitting under the gazebo and on the patio. I did not have to prepare or cook meals, because we could eat at our favorite restaurants. Truly, this was a blessing and a delightful change! We would go on short walks around the hotel, praying and holding hands. Most mornings, my husband would sit and enjoy the wide window view from the roof top room with beautiful palm trees swishing in the wind, as he watched the heavenly view of God's Creation, in the clouds during the day, and the moon and the stars at night. He could witness the beautiful sunrise in the morning and glorious sunset in the evening. No, we were not in Hawaii, or Florida, but a Hilton hotel, in Georgia!

Interestingly enough, during these months, my husband became more alert and active. He enjoyed every minute of our stay. I guess we got our "Honeymoon Suite", after all. Our "*first* honeymoon" was a local fishing trip, with our son, but our "*last* honeymoon" was at a beautiful hotel, with ("Just the two of us") in a very small hotel room where the service was great and the people were very accommodating. What a blessing! I will never forget Room 233.

Another blessing came our way, in the midst of all of our challenges and storms. However, in the midst of it all, we had a major storm when one of our grandchildren strayed away in darkness, but life is such that we try to teach our children about life, Jesus, salvation, training them in the right way that they should go, praying that they get it, and sometimes they do, but many times they don't. In spite of these circumstances, it does not make God any less of a heavenly Father, or us any less as parents or grandparents, especially when we have done our best to show and teach them about God, His Creation, and life. I could very well have left this out, but the Bible teaches us about life, and God included all family matters in His word, no matter how heartbreaking and disheartening, because He wants us and others to grow, and to learn how and how not to, live, that we might live the abundant life, as we bring glory to His name. It is our prayer that in some miraculous way, even in this, God's name may be glorified, for He is a "*Good Father*", who still has unconditional love for us, and still sees us as "His own."

Yes, our family was truly saddened, as we weathered this storm, but all we can do when our family members or (even we ourselves) make ungodly decisions and choose evil over good, and darkness over light is hope and pray that we all will do what King David did in *Psalm 51.* We must cry out! *"Have mercy upon me O God, I acknowledge my transgressions, I confess my sins, o purge me, create in me a clean heart, and renew a right spirit within me, knowing that, while we were yet sinners, Christ died for us. Romans 5:8*

As a family, we are yet united in prayer continually, for all who were affected and asking that our "seed" would experience "godly sorrow" which produces repentance leading to salvation not to be regretted, because we know that the "sorrow of the world" produces death, but repentance brings freedom... *II Corinthians 7:10-11*

Consequently, we continue to pray for our "seed", because we are yet producing others. For in the midst of this storm, we were blessed with two granddaughters (in law), (Jayda Simmons Moss/ *Kahlil),* and (Ashlee Dixon Ezell/*Antonio, Jr.),* along with two great-grandchildren, Aria Denise Ezell (Alexis), and Rapha' El Lavi Ezell (Antonio, Jr).

I am convinced that throughout life, we all will experience times of challenges and storms of *sin, sorrow, sickness, suffering and death.* In this world, they will forever be present with us all. However, we must fight and press on trusting and believing in our Creator, while counting our blessings. We must choose righteousness, because whoever pursues righteousness and love finds life, prosperity, and honor. *Proverbs 21:21* However, I must say that I am one of the first to admit that sometimes, this is not always easy.

I have a family saying, that I use sometimes, "Living life the E-Z (Ezell)Way has not always been *E-A-S-Y."* But through it all, as a family, we have had to stand strong, fight wars both inside and out and as we continue to live, while still sharing many great laughs and happy memories! I wanted to share several of them, but those laughs and other *fierce* challenges are reserved for another book.

Nevertheless, just for laughs, I will share this particular one, because according to my eldest son (Don), from this experience, he and his siblings learned a valuable lesson *in "delayed gratification."* And it also, taught them a lesson about *sacrifice and choice.*

Now, on with our story!

One year, we experienced a Christmas, which our children said they would never forget. With limited funds, due to job losses, after a family forum, they had to choose between a new car or four new Go-carts. Much to our surprise, they chose the "new car", instead of the "four shiny red Go-Carts." Seriously!

However, that Christmas morning, they were *highly disappointed* when all they found under the tree was a *measly $25.00* in a Christmas card. But then we took them outside, where they saw a beautiful new shiny black 1986 Bonneville *(beige leather seats)* with *a big red bow*. And they were so excited! Later on, they were even more excited because, for summer vacation, we all traveled to *Disneyland in Florida* and for the first time, we were able to ride comfortably in our family car.

For over the years past, as a family of six, we had traveled by car to *Six Flags, Lion Country Safari, Grant's Park Zoo, Stone Mountain, Indian Springs, High Falls,* and several other places in Georgia, in our small car, which was a little *canary yellow Volkswagen* which we nicknamed, *"Tweety Bird."* But after the new car purchase, we could spread our wings and we ventured out to other states and visited *Sea World, Bush Gardens, Look-Out Mountain, King's Dominion, Alabama Shipyard, Washington DC, New York, New Jersey, Maryland, and Philadelphia.*

As I reflect upon all of our challenges, illnesses, and financial crises, I am convinced that all of our good times really outweighed our bad times. How did we even afford to take them to all of those places? I now know that it was only by the grace of God! And on that note, I must end my revised version with a continuation of the last line in our first book. **Psalm 71:19** *God, you have done great things!*

O God, who is like You?

Thus, the *"revised"* version of our book, is written to testify to God's never ending unfailing love, mercy, grace, kindness, goodness, righteousness and judgment, and to declare that there is victory in Christ Jesus for all who view life in the Spirit of our Lord and Savior Jesus Christ through the providential and sovereign lens of God Almighty, our Creator.

<u>Therefore, the end and sum of our life story is this:</u>
You who have shown me great and severe troubles,
Shall revive me again,
And bring me up again from the depths of the earth.
You shall increase my greatness,
And comfort me on every side. **Psalm 71:20-21**

Much Love,
<u>*Retha Evans Ezell*</u>

APPENDIX
MARRIAGE MANIFESTO

So, God created man in His own image; in the image of God created He him; male and female created He them.

Then God blessed them, and God said to them, be fruitful, and multiply; fill the earth, and subdue it: have dominion over the fish of the sea, the birds of the air, and over every living thing that moves on the earth. **Genesis 1:27-28**

And the Lord caused a deep sleep to fall on Adam, and he slept; and He took one of his ribs, and closed up the flesh in its place. Then the rib which the Lord God had taken from man He made into a woman, and He brought her to the man. And Adam said, this is now bone of my bones and flesh of my flesh; she shall be called Woman because she was taken from a Man. **Genesis 2:21-23**

He who finds a wife finds a good thing, and obtains favor from the Lord. **Proverbs 18:22**

Wives, submit to your own husbands as to the Lord. **Ephesians 5:22**

Husbands love your wives, just as Christ also loved the church and gave Himself for her. **Ephesians 5:25**

Children, obey your parents in the Lord, for this is right. **Ephesians 6:1**

Likewise, ye husbands, dwell with them according to knowledge, giving Honor unto the wife, as unto the wife, as unto the weaker vessel, and as being heirs together of the grace of life; that your prayers be not hindered. **KJV**

For husbands, this means love your wives, just as Christ loved the church. **Ephesians 5:25**

House and riches are an inheritance from the fathers, but a prudent wife is from the Lord. **Proverbs 19:14**

Let the husband render unto the wife the affection due her, and likewise, the wife unto the husband. **I Corinthians 7:3 KJV**

For the husband is the head of the wife, even as Christ is the head of the church: and he is the savior of the body. **Ephesians 5:23 KJV**

For this reason, a man will leave his father and mother and be joined to his wife, and the two shall become one flesh. **Ephesians 5:31**

Husbands love your wives, and be not bitter toward them. **Colossians 3:19 KJV**

Moses because of the hardness of your hearts suffered you to put away your wives: but from the beginning, it was not so. **Matthew 19:8 KJV**

For the unbelieving husband is sanctified by the wife, and the unbelieving wife is sanctified by the husband, otherwise your children would be unclean, but now they are holy.
I Corinthians 7:14

Let your fountain be blessed: and rejoice with the wife of your youth. **Proverbs 5:18**

DID YOU KNOW?

God has a plan and purpose for every life. **Jeremiah 1:4-5, 29:11, Psalm 139:14-16, Matthew 1:21, John 3:16**

God put people together in some of the most unusual ways and places. **Isaiah 55:8-9, Luke:2:5-7, Exodus 2:3**

Sometimes God has to move us to use us. **Genesis 12:1-2, Genesis 39:1, Exodus 3&4, John 3:16, Acts 9:9-10,**

You can be blessed even through trials and afflictions. **Genesis 39:4 I Kings 17, Luke 24:46-51, James 1:2-4**

You are never without a father because your heavenly Father is with you always. **Hebrews 13:5-13, Matthew 6:5-13, Matthew 28:19-20**

In life, we sometimes make bad choices but with God, we can make things right by repentance, and confession of our Lord and Savior Jesus Christ. **Romans 10:9-13, John 3:16, I John 1:9-10, II Corinthians 7:10-12**

If you marry someone who has a deep sense of family, they will probably have good family sense. **Proverbs 10:1, Exodus 20:12, Ephesians 6:4, I Peter 4:8-11**

All sickness is not unto death. **II Kings 20:4-6, John 11:4, John 11:25**

Life and death are in the hands of God. **Deuteronomy 32:39, Romans 8:38, Jeremiah 21:8**

All things work together for good when we love God. **Romans 8:28, Ephesians 3:20**

God uses husbands and wives as co-laborers in His vineyard. **Acts 18:1-3, I Corinthians 16:9**

God has ordained marriage for ministry.

Genesis 1:21-24, Genesis 16:1-6, Ruth 1-4, Acts 18:1-3

MARRIAGE
(Q.U.I.C.K.)

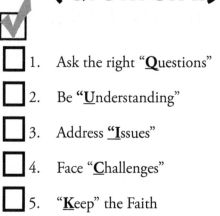

☐ 1.   Ask the right "**Q**uestions"

☐ 2.   Be "**U**nderstanding"

☐ 3.   Address "**I**ssues"

☐ 4.   Face "**C**hallenges"

☐ 5.   "**K**eep" the Faith

So, then, they are no longer two, but one flesh. Therefore, what God has joined together, let no one separate. **Matthew 19:6**

SESSION ONE (pages 39- 50)

1. How did you meet your spouse?
2. Were you both childhood sweethearts?
3. How long did you date before marriage?
4. Who were your childhood friends?
5. Were any of them instrumental in your meeting your spouse?

A friend loveth at all times... **Proverbs 17:17**

SESSION TWO (pages 57- 64)

1. What wrong choices did you make, during your teen years?
2. What were the consequences?
3. What did you learn from your experiences?
4. Did any of your wrong choices affect your marriage?
5. Did you have to take care of any family members?
6. If so, how did this affect your marriage?
7. Have these experiences helped you to minister to others?

Now we exhort you, brethren, warn them who are unruly, comfort the fainthearted, uphold the weak; and be patient with all. **I Thessalonians 5:14**

SESSION THREE (pages 73, 89, 92- 95)

1. Did you have a formal wedding? Why/Why not?
2. Did you have premarital counseling, "*before*" becoming engaged and setting your date for marriage?
3. Where did you spend your honeymoon?
4. Did you live with your in-laws, at any time, during marriage?
5. If so, what challenges did you face?
6. Do you own your own home? Why/why not?

Listen to counsel, and receive instruction, that you may be wise in your latter days. There are many plans in a man's heart, nevertheless, the Lord's counsel-that will stand.
Proverbs 19:20-21

SESSION FOUR (pages 73- 88)

1. Do you have children?
2. Did you have children before marriage?
3. If so, did this affect your marriage?
4. How many children did you both want?
5. How many children did you have?
6. If you didn't have children, did it affect your marriage?
7. Do you have a blended family?
8. Has this affected your marriage?
9. What helpful advice could you give others?

Children are a heritage, and the fruit of the womb is a reward.
Psalm 127:3

SESSION FIVE (pages 89- 100)

1. Were you and your spouse financially stable when you married?
2. Have you faced any major financial hardships, since marriage?
3. Has your financial stability increased or decreased, since marriage?
4. Do you have a financial plan?
5. What advice could you give others in managing their finances and becoming good stewards?
6. Do you have joint bank accounts? Why/Why not?

And you shall remember the Lord your God, for it is He who gives you power to get wealth, that He may establish His covenant which He swore to your fathers, as it is this day.
Deuteronomy 8:18

SESSION SIX (pages 101- 130)

1. Have you or your spouse experienced any major illnesses, during your marriage?
2. Do you have a family health and nutrition plan?
3. Do you have annual check-ups?
4. Have you ever experienced the loss of a loved one?
5. How did you cope with family crises and challenges?
6. How do you handle issues and conflict?
7. Do you and your husband "talk"?

For bodily exercise profits little, but godliness is profitable for all things, having promise of the life that now is and of that which is to come... for to this end we both labor and suffer reproach, because we trust in the living God.
   I Timothy 4:8

SESSION SEVEN (pages 25, 30, 92- 100)

1. Have you ever felt like throwing in the "marriage towel?"
2. Were you or your spouse's parents divorced?
3. If so, how did this affect your marriage?
4. Did you grow up without a father or mother in the home?
5. If so, did this affect your marriage?
6. Do you and your spouse have a "deep sense" of family?
7. Did you have any issues of unfaithfulness?
8. If so, did you recover?
9. Did you have a "Covenant Marriage Ceremony?"

So then, they are no longer two but one flesh. Therefore, what God has joined together, let no man separate.
   Matthew 19:6

SESSION EIGHT (pages 131- 178)

1. Do you and your spouse share the same faith?
2. Do you and your spouse pray together and attend church services together on a regular basis?
3. Has your faith increased or decreased, since marriage?"
4. Have you and/or your spouse been called into a particular ministry?
5. If so, into what ministry have you been called?
6. Do you believe that marriage is God-ordained for His purpose?

*Two are better than one because they have a good reward for their labor. For if they fall, one will lift up his companion. **Ecclesiastes 4:9-10***

ACKNOWLEDGMENTS

I must express my sincere thanks and gratitude to all of those who made this most exhilarating endeavor possible. The life experiences that tell our story also encompass the story of those who have traveled through life with us, thus far. Many have experienced our joys. Some have even shared in our pain. Truly, God had our paths to cross for His own divine purpose. And for this, I am filled with gratitude and heartfelt thanks. I thank you all for being there for us, and for your love and fervent prayers, especially, Pastor James and Linda R. Callaway (Eric, William Randall, Capt. Timothy C. Moore), (Dr. Jane E. Thomas and Nekeisha Randall), (Cassandra White Haire), and our ("Genesis One" Marriage Disciples) Robert and Donna Jenkins.

But above all, we thank our church family, Springhill Community Church of the Living God, for those who were faithful to the end and supported us in ministry for over thirty **(30)** years, as we served as pastor, Co-Pastor, then bishop and apostle. We pray that you stay strong and continue in the work and ministry, which the living God started through us and you.

A very special thank you to the late Dr. William E. Schatten, who through his divine wisdom and skillful hands, was able to mend my husband's health. God used him as His vessel to preserve my husband's life and because of this, we are here together writing our life story. Without his work, our story would have ended over thirty-seven **(37)** years ago.

So today, by the grace of God, my husband was by my side inspiring and encouraging me to finish this revised work. From the beginning to now, he was an integral part of this journey. Through his endearing love and humble spirit, I was able to make the necessary changes needed to make this <u>"Our Story."</u> He was also instrumental in assisting me in the preparation and publication of penning the most significant events of our life together even unto the end.

I am also especially indebted to my daughter-in-law Tamyala Clarke Ezell (Tammy) who said, *"Write the words down so others may read it"* and in the revised version, to the late Bro. Henry Slocumb (who was my husband's dear friend), one who would send a word to me every Wednesday after DQ Bible Study, *"Tell Rete, It is time to write another book!"* To Fox Valley Printing and my cousin, Lola Morrow, for her sketches from long ago. Also, words cannot express my gratitude and respect for my editor LaChandra Fitzgerald (My goddaughter) whose exceptional skills helped to integrate the experiences in our first edition, which also helped the revised edition flow smoothly. I offer heartfelt gratitude to my family friends, Valincenia Griggs Shannon, who previewed my first draft and *Phil, Frenardo, Valescia,* who all shared in and recalled significant events in our lives. We offer special love, blessings and prayers, to our in-laws, Richard/*Zenobia Hodges (Kelvin* and *Fredena),* Geraldine Clark (Tammy/ *Jacques),* and to all our many other supportive families, friends, and ministers of the gospel at home and abroad.

In this very special season of our lives, I would like to offer a "Special Tribute" to the late Bishop John A. Moss (July 27, 2023) and his lovely wife Pastor Naydean Robinson Moss, (our son-in law Dahl/*Val*) Moss's father and mother, (our neighbor and friend), who were also married for over fifty-one (**51**) years and ministered *together faithfully* in God's vineyard (Faith Temple, Cochran, GA) for well over thirty (**30**) years (just as my husband and I did), as they carried out their marriage vows, <u>"until death do, we part."</u>

Lastly, I am deeply grateful to "Inspiring Voices" who encouraged, assisted, and supported us in finishing our first edition of **"Love Leaps Forward, Time Tilts Backward"**, and a very special thank you to "Readers Magnet" for journeying with us, as we finished the good work that God had already begun. ***Philippians 1:6*** We are forever indebted to you all.

The Late Bishop James Calvin Ezell
Apostle Retha Evans Ezell

Special Acknowledgment

In Loving Memory

Then we who are alive and remain shall be caught up together with them in the clouds to meet the Lord in the air. And thus we shall always be with the lord. *First Thessalonians 4:17*

Elder Robert Alfred Ezell (Primitive Baptist Church)/ Ozie Bell Stanley Ezell (Parents of James Calvin Ezell)

Freddye Bell Ezell Minton/Richard, Barbara-Bobbie Ruth Ezell Jarrell/Charles (Siblings)

Young Calvin Evans/Rosa Napier Evans (Parents of Retha Evans Ezell)

Winfred, Alfonzo, Alvin, Calvin (Infant) Siblings Beloved Aunt (Dorothy Stanley Thomas), Aunt Freeman, Arthur Ragin, Sr. (Uncle Jack) and children (Lucille Nottingham, Lola Morrow, Rose and Arthur Ragin, Jr.

Agnue (Buddy)/Fleter Dawson White (Crystal) Parents

Nathaniel Clarke (Tamyala) Parent

With all our love,

Children

Grandchildren

Great Grandchildren

and

The many generations to come!

"And I will establish My covenant between Me and thee and thy seed after thee in their generations for an everlasting covenant, to be a God unto thee and to thy seed after thee.
Genesis 17:7 KJV

Now unto Him who is able to do exceedingly abundantly above all that we ask or think, according to the power that worketh in us, unto Him be glory in the church by Christ Jesus throughout all ages, world without end. **KJV** Amen
Ephesians 3:20-21 KJV

Blessed is He that readeth, and they that hear the words of this prophecy, and keep those things which are written therein: for the time is at hand. **Revelation 1:3 KJV**

To God Be the Glory; All the Glory Be to God!

Printed in the USA
CPSIA information can be obtained
at www.ICGtesting.com
LVHW010130081224
798392LV00015B/484